Dateline Vermont

DATELINE VERMONT

Covering and uncovering the stories, big and small, that shaped a state — and influenced a nation

CHRIS GRAFF

Former Vermont bureau chief for The Associated Press

THISTLE HILL PUBLICATIONS
North Pomfret, Vermont

Published by Thistle Hill Publications
Post Office Box 307, North Pomfret, Vermont 05053
802.457.2050
www.thistlehillpub.com
Jack Crowl, publisher

ISBN-10: 0-9705511-3-4
ISBN-13: 978-0-9705511-3-9

Library of Congress Control Number: 2006909047

Printed in Canada

To my mother, Patricia Graff McCord,
and my stepfather, Bert McCord,
whose marriage brought me to Vermont,
and to my children, Garrett and Lindsay,
who will always be Vermonters.

Contents

Vote four McMullen

Editorial cartoonist Jeff Danziger tweaks failed senatorial candidiate Jack McMullen.

Introduction

"How many teats does a cow have?"

Perhaps never has a Vermont political campaign fallen apart so quickly. One week before the 1998 primary election, Republican U.S. Senate candidates Fred Tuttle and Jack McMullen met in a debate on Vermont Public Radio in a format that allowed the candidates to ask each other questions.

"Jack, let's start off easy. What's a tedder?" asked Tuttle, a folksy farmer from Tunbridge who looked like someone who hawks oatmeal.

"I have no idea," said a startled McMullen, a businessman who had moved to the state from Massachusetts just a year before.

"You have no idea? It's a hay tedder that tosses the hay up so you can get it dry," explained Tuttle. Next he asked McMullen to define rowen (the second cutting of hay). Again, McMullen had no answer. Finally, Tuttle asked McMullen how many teats a cow has. McMullen said six; the correct answer is four.

Up until this point, listeners probably thought the whole exchange was amusing but unimportant, as the native Tuttle, not nearly the hayseed he appeared, tried to imprint the carpetbagger label on McMullen. But then Tuttle handed McMullen a short list of Vermont communities and asked him to read the names aloud. The candidate fell back on his French to pronounce Calais and learned like many others before him that a little knowledge can be a dangerous thing. In Vermont everyone knows it's pronounced "callous." Always has been, always will. McMullen did no better with Leicester. Finally, desperate to show that he had at least a basic sense of the state's geography, McMullen recited the names of Vermont's fourteen counties, something every Vermont grade schooler learns to do in the fourth grade.

If there was any life in the McMullen candidacy, it died that night. Tuttle, whose candidacy started out as a publicity stunt for the low-budget film "Man With A Plan," defeated McMullen in the Republican primary. In a race that progressed from film to live farce, Tuttle went on to endorse incumbent Democrat Patrick Leahy in the November election. That voters would give the nomination to the 79-year-old Tuttle, a tenth-grade dropout who had had three heart attacks and prostate cancer, was nearly blind in one eye, and hobbled around on two canes, says much about the quirky world of Vermont politics.

The state Republican Party, humiliated by McMullen's self destruction and Tuttle's growing popularity, challenged Tuttle's nominating petitions. The secretary of state ruled that the Tunbridge farmer needed an additional 23 nominating signatures. He came back with 2,300.

McMullen was baffled: Why would voters favor a self-described frivolous candidate over someone who planned to give Leahy a real run for his money. "I have done my homework," McMullen protested. "I've spent seventeen-hour days meeting with hundreds and hundreds of people around the state. I've spent a lot of time learning about the issues." And he had. Vermont voters, though, look at more than policy position papers when they choose candidates. In 1998 they were apparently more interested in milk than whine.

People who live in and around the Green Mountains have believed that Vermont is a special world since well before *Vermont Life* slapped that title on a book thirty-eight years ago and started making money off it. Vermonters, in fact, have been marketing the state as a unique place since the decades after the Civil War. During those rough years of rapid industrialization and urbanization, urbanites throughout the Northeast started looking for a place they could use as an escape. The idea that Vermont is a special place, therefore, goes back about 150 years. It's an idea so entrenched that most Vermonters believe fervently that the state can't be understood after a year or two or five or ten. Something about this state doesn't come to light easily or quickly. Tuttle, whose face was once described as "Vermont's face — all harsh winters and rocky resilience"— became a symbol of that heritage.

Tuttle provided lots of laughs in that campaign. Asked how serious he was about running, he replied, "Well, I can't run too fast." Asked if he was too old for the job, he said, "I'm a little bit old for anything." And, of course, there was his favorite plank in his platform: More girlie shows at the state fair!

To dismiss Fred Tuttle's appeal as comic relief is a mistake. As a journalist, I've had the privilege of charting Vermont's political course for the past thirty years. I've witnessed the dissolution of more than one political campaign run by candidates who believed that the office was theirs as long as they threw enough money into the fray. I have also witnessed the quiet dignity of Emory Hebard, who served for years as a competent state treasurer, running every two years by handing out to every constituent he met a card to which he had attached a shiny new penny to stress his fiscal conservatism. (Of course, Hebard had to stop when someone complained to the secretary of state that he was buying votes.) I've covered Jim Jeffords' departure from the Republican Party in 2001 and Howard Dean's presidential campaign from its humble beginnings.

But I have also had the privilege of covering much more than elections. I've covered thirty years of Vermont town meetings, dozens of droughts and an equal number of floods, several dairy compacts, school refinancing, and environmental reform. I've covered civil disobedience, civil unions, and the moving civil discourse of fulltime Vermonters who were willing to work part time and for little pay to try to do what was meet and right for the state.

Early legislatures I covered used to stop the clock just before midnight on the grueling Saturday nights when they finished the session's work. Until all the compromises were finally worked out between the House and Senate, the hands on the clock did not move. Only when all the "i's" were dotted and the "t's" crossed on the session's legislation was the clock restarted so the governor could give the closing statement at the day's contrived end. It was a neat trick, but it didn't fool anyone. Time does not stand still. Change is a constant. Half of this job I loved was to spot the change, document it and analyze it. The other half was to keep an eye on Vermont's essence and make sure it was not forgotten in the name of progress. I have been honored to be a witness to life in the state I love.

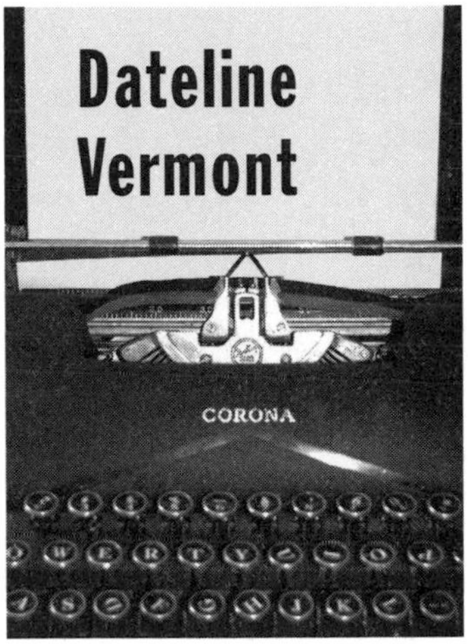
Dateline
Vermont
CORONA

Phil Hoff celebrates his 1962 election as Vermont's first Democratic governor since the Civil War.

"One hundred years of bondage —broken!"

— Gov. Phil Hoff

Chapter 1

The Difficult 1960s

I came to Vermont in 1965 when we were both going through difficult times. It was July, and I was eleven. My father had died suddenly the previous October, and my mother had remarried only seven months later, anxious about having three children to rear. My mother had met this man nineteen years earlier at my parents' wedding, but I had met him only once, in February, when we had been invited up ostensibly to ski and in truth to meet the man who would soon become my stepfather. He lived on a gentleman's farm near the end of a dirt road in North Pomfret, outside Woodstock. Now it was July, and my eighteen-year-old sister, off to college in the fall, was driving me north from Westport, Connecticut, my home until then and home to all my friends. My brother, destined to leave for prep school at the end of the summer and mired in an Elvis Presley phase, would be along shortly.

My sister and I took the new interstate as far as it went—which was Bellows Falls at that time—and then traveled on progressively rural roads until one dirt road finally petered out at the foot of a squat hill. My sister pulled into the second driveway from the end of Caper Street, a name that had a ridiculously suburban ring to it, but I thought I'd just arrived at the end of the world.

A month earlier, the Vermont Legislature had adopted court-ordered reapportionment. Since its organization as a state in 1791, Vermont had clung to a system of one town-one vote, despite the fact that by the mid 1960s the town of Stannard, population 113, tucked away in the Northeast Kingdom, remained as powerful in the House as the city of Burlington, with its 35,000 residents. Many Vermonters thought it unconscionable that representatives of twelve percent of the population could control a majority vote in the 246-member House, but nothing changed until a federal judge ordered reapportionment. Throughout the 1965 session, lawmakers worked out an agreement on a 150-member House that would be apportioned according to population.

The agreement, however, did not herald universal support and acceptance of this important change. Many legislators from smaller towns took the loss of their town's influence hard. Frank Hutchins represented Stannard. He wept on the floor of the House as he condemned the outsiders in the Legislature (meaning those who had recently moved to the state) who "come into our parlors and try to change things." His colleague from Pownal, James Lounsbury, called it "symbolic that freedom and Jesus Christ both died at three o'clock on a Friday afternoon."

And there were other ominous signs of difficult change. Just a year earlier, Romaine Tenney had watched with growing desperation as bulldozers, heavy trucks, explosives and an army of men carved out the path of an interstate highway in Vermont. Working their way north from the Massachusetts border and oblivious to mountains and valleys, they drew ever nearer to his Ascutney farm. His family had been on that land since 1892, and Tenney still ploughed with horses and hayed with a pitchfork. When the work crew reached his farm, Tenney refused to leave. Finally, a sheriff appeared with a court order and his own army of five workers to begin emptying old tools and harnesses from one of the sheds. They worked until dark and then quit, but they planned to return in the morning to finish the job. A few hours later, however, Howard Fitch was driving his babysitter home when he noticed a strange glow from Old Man Tenney's place. Fitch raced to the fire station and pulled the alarm, but it was too late. Romaine Tenney had vowed, "I was born here and I'll die here," and he did, because he knew the interstate would change Vermont irrevocably, just as reapportionment would.

And there were other ominous signs of difficult change. Just a year earlier, Romaine Tenney had watched with growing desperation as bulldozers, heavy trucks, explosives and an army of men carved out the path of an interstate highway in Vermont.

But in some cases, the lack of change was as hard to bear as the change. If the phrase "Vermont is a Third-World Country" had been uttered yet, and if I had been old enough to take its meaning, I would have agreed. In my mind, no country portrayed in *National Geographic* looked more remote and less inviting than North Pomfret. Ironically, looking around from the vantage point of my new home on an abandoned, isolated hill farm in Vermont, I saw exactly what Frank Hutchins and Romaine Tenney had seen, and like them, I cried, but for different reasons. I was an eleven-year-old adolescent with an unusual amount on my plate, and they were the last of a generation deep in grief for what was being lost. I mourned my situation by wearing a black armband every day, but in time, thanks to my stepfather's love and patience, I began to come around to the opposite side of the fence.

My stepfather, Bert McCord, came to Vermont for everything I couldn't see, for the beauty and qualities Hutchins and Tenney wanted to protect. Originally a journalist and then later, for a long time, a drama critic for the now defunct New York *Herald Tribune*, he retired early and left the starlets and late nights to move to Vermont in 1958. He bought a failing, hundred-acre hill farm and kept it as a gentleman's farm, digging a four-acre pond, tending a big vegetable garden and hiring the farmer at the end of the road to hay the fields to keep them open. A pair of two-hundred-year-old maples towered over the 1848 farmhouse, and the view from the kitchen stoop across at least two mountain ranges was unmarred by any human construction. It took a while for me to appreciate all this—for a long time, it just seemed lonely—but I came to see and cherish this as one of the most beautiful spots anywhere. For roughly forty years it was my anchor, and when my stepfather and mother died many years later, I held on to ten acres because even now I cannot bear to lose that connection.

> ...my stepfather was a careful man with a deliberate teaching style. Under his tutelage, I began to learn about Vermont's special qualities and character, and about writing, as well, all of which became critical when I eventually became a Vermont journalist.

Bert's longtime friends from Broadway wondered what he did in Vermont. He replied that he wrote checks, but truly he reveled in the rural world. Each year he marked on a calendar the day of the first sap run, the day the ice went out on the pond, the day the bluebirds returned to the house beyond the terrace wall, the day the phoebes arrived to build their nest above the kitchen stoop, the instant the black flies hatched, the day of the first peas and the last lettuce. Early on these milestones seemed like dandelion fluff beside the action I'd known in Westport— sailing, for example, which I'd learned from my father—but my stepfather was a careful man with a deliberate teaching style. Under his tutelage, I began to learn about Vermont's special qualities and character, and about writing, as well, all of which became critical when I eventually became a Vermont journalist.

Harold Harrington built the farmhouse at the end of our road around 1900—they called it Echo Farm—and his son, Norman, had been working with his father since he graduated in 1948 from the Vermont School of Agriculture, in Randolph. Norman, whose friends called him "Clown," stopped by my house almost every day to visit, drop off fresh eggs and discuss the weather. He and Bert were an odd couple, but they unconsciously taught me a great deal about the new and the old Vermont. They spent every Sunday in the fall in our parlor watching the usually hapless New York Giants on television while the pungent odor of silage, which followed Norman everywhere, filled the house. He played basketball with me at the town hall and taught me how to drive a tractor and hay the fields. He took my brother coon hunting with his dog, Rebel.

When my brother was home from prep school, we'd go up and visit with Harold for hours on end, eating popcorn slathered with his home-made butter. Too old to farm, he would entertain us by singing old ballads such as "The Hartford Wreck," which tells the tragic story of the horrific wreck of a central Vermont railroad passenger train. All the passengers died when the cars plunged off the Hartford bridge.

> *Twas the Montreal express*
> *It was speeding at its best*
> *When on Hartford bridge it struck a broken rail.*
> *To the river with a crash*
> *That ill-fated train was dashed.*
> *One hundred souls went down to meet their fate.*

One of my favorite songs was a poignant love song for the state:

> *The orchard on the hill.*
> *I think I see it still.*
> *Back among the dear green hills of old Vermont.*

I was young and full of myself, but after listening to Harold, even I could see that Vermont was changing.

Sometimes that change was slow. North Pomfret in 1965 was like much of Vermont: rural and Republican. Most of the town's roads were dirt. A special ring on the town's party line alerted the volunteer firefighters to where the fire was. The post office doubled as the general store, and both were run by Stuart Harrington, another member of that sprawling local family. We had a series of one-room schoolhouses for elementary grades, but students in seventh and eighth grades rode buses every day to Woodstock Elementary School.

In 1972 my godfather, Otis Guernsey, who also lived in North Pomfret, tried to establish a North Pomfret Democratic Committee. He roped my stepfather into serving as treasurer and called a meeting at the South Pomfret Schoolhouse for February 29. The McCords, the Guernseys, and four other people showed up. To prime the pump, each person agreed to contribute one dollar, so Bert was put in charge of a treasury of eight dollars. Unfortunately for those who thought state government might benefit from a little ideological diversity, a mailing to Pomfret voters later in the year resulted in many of the letters being returned with comments such as, "Sorry, Bub, wrong party" and "I believe in a two-party system and will support the Republican Party any way I can."

> The bond between Vermont and the Republican Party grew out of a dislike for slavery and a strong belief in the sanctity of the union of states. That philosophy meshed well with small-town, rural life. Powering it was a GOP machine that organized to win elections without fail.

My own introduction to state government came in 1967, when my Woodstock Elementary School eighth-grade class traveled to visit the State House. Phil Hoff, a Democrat who had shocked the state by being elected governor in 1962, the first Democrat to hold that office since the Civil War, took the time to greet us and shake hands. Dick Mallary, then the speaker of the House, gave a short talk. But what I remember most vividly about that first trip north to see the workings of government is the men's bathroom in the basement. The room is huge; the fixtures brass, the countertops marble. Its lavish decoration clearly belied its lowly purpose. I was so impressed that I took photographs (and still have them).

Years later, when my wife wrote a short history of the State House, I learned that the bathroom had been installed at the order of legislators in 1884. They were weary of tramping out behind the building to the outhouses. No comparable facility was installed for women. There wasn't any need. There weren't any women in the State House.

I was only thirteen on that field trip so I might be forgiven for missing the point of it, but clearly I was impressed by the wrong thing. Hoff's election five years earlier had stunned the state and won national attention. Only Republicans had won the office of governor since Stephen Royce was elected in 1854 as a Whig-Republican and re-elected in 1855 as a Republican. Between the 1850s and 1950s, Vermont was sometimes nearly alone in the depth of its support for Republicans. In 1912 only Vermont and Utah supported the presidential bid of William Howard Taft; in 1936 Vermont and Maine were the only states to vote against Franklin D. Roosevelt.

The bond between Vermont and the Republican Party grew out of a dislike for slavery and a strong belief in the sanctity of the union of states. That philosophy meshed well with small-town, rural life. Powering it was a GOP machine that organized to win elections without fail. Starting in the 1870s, the Proctor family assumed a leadership role that allowed it to run the state, with a few interruptions, for some eighty years.

Politics in this controlled environment were predictable. Politicians climbed a ladder, serving as speaker of the House, lieutenant governor and then governor in a pre-determined sequence that for most of a century included a rotation between the western and eastern sides of the state that became known as the Mountain Rule. It is remarkable, in retrospect, that this alternating pattern prevailed for so long and through the inevitable dust-ups in politics that were bound to crop up even in a one-party state.

B ut change, of which I later represented one iota, began sweeping into Vermont in the 1950s. The interstates put Vermont within easy reach; the ski areas and the heavy marketing of Vermont as the beckoning country enticed many; a new IBM plant in Essex brought in thousands of new residents, as did the state's growing colleges and universities. Many graduates simply stayed on. Quality of life was increasingly important to people all across the country. And that was something Vermont could offer.

Democrats recognized the changing demographics — and they responded: Beginning with the gubernatorial campaign of Robert Larrow in 1952, the Democrats began serious efforts to capture political office. In 1958 William Meyer became the first Democratic congressman from Vermont; that year's gubernatorial contest was so close it required a recount. Finally, in 1962, three years before I arrived in the state, Philip Hoff rode the popularity of President Kennedy and hammered home the theme that a century was too long for one party to rule. He won as governor, defeating the incumbent. That election night in 1962 was a watershed moment in Vermont politics. As the final votes showed Hoff winning, he instinctively returned to those who had put him over the top: the people of Winooski.

Hoff stood on the front seat of an open convertible, grinning from ear to ear and reaching out to a cheering crowd in a scene that looked nearly religious in its zeal. The roars of these working class supporters echoed off the mills that made up the heavily Democratic city. People filled the streets even though it was so late at night that it was actually morning. Hoff responded to the roars; his outstretched arms spanned the car.

"One hundred years of bondage — broken!" he shouted.

Here was a great politician who had scaled a hitherto unimaginable height in Vermont.

But when I met him that day in the State House in 1967, I didn't know any of this. What I took away from that visit to the symbol of Vermont government was amazement at the extravagant bathroom. The seat of government might be upstairs, in the governor's office or perhaps the House chamber, but down here in the basement was where they hid the thrones.

Chris Graff in the Senate chamber at the State House, 1978.

"I am not sure which came first— my love of politics or of journalism."

— Chris Graff

Chapter 2

An Education in Politics and Reporting

I never knew Winston Prouty, but his death played a big part in my life. Prouty, a U.S. senator from Vermont, died September 10, 1971. I had just arrived at Middlebury College as a freshman and was sitting outside the student center, which housed the college's thriving radio station, WRMC-FM. The news director of the station walked by looking for volunteers to help cover Prouty's funeral, which was going to be held on the 15th. He and I had met briefly at the college's activity fair for freshmen, when I had wandered over to the radio station's table. Now he told me that he wanted coverage starting at the Burlington airport, where delegations from the U.S. Senate and House would arrive on a special flight from Andrews Air Force Base, and continuing along the route from Burlington to Newport, where the memorial service would be held. After that he wanted full coverage of the service itself at the United Church of Newport.

These seemed even to me at the time to be pretty ambitious plans for a small, non-commercial college radio station, but I would learn soon enough that this news director was full of ambitious plans. His name was Jim Douglas. A year later, at the age of 21, he would be elected to the state House of Representatives; 31 years later he would be elected governor. On that September day, though, I was an eager convert ready to go wherever I was needed, and he led me into the world of broadcast journalism and gave me my first assignment.

Jim was an impressive figure, even then. He has an amazing broadcast voice, and he and his partner, fellow senior Scott Harmon, anchored the evening news on WRMC-FM with the skill and delivery of NBC's Huntley and Brinkley. Sometimes, though, Jim had trouble turning off his broadcast voice. One time he stood in for U.S. Rep. Richard Mallary at a 1974 debate for the U.S. Senate held at the college. Jim read Mallary's statement on the environment in the same sonorous tones in which he delivered the news. That prompted some friendly laughter from the audience, which he acknowledged by concluding with, "and we'll have the weather next." Jim has always had a surprisingly and underappreciated dry sense of humor and a quick wit. In one of the college's auditoriums, the radio station several times hosted "The Room Mate Game," a live spoof on the classic television game show, "The Dating Game." Jim always played the host and came up with hilarious, irreverent questions that belied his persona as one of the most conservative students on campus. To this day, he remains a master of innuendo.

> These [ideas] seemed even to me at the time to be pretty ambitious plans for a small, non-commercial college radio station, but I would learn soon enough that this news director was full of ambitious plans. His name was Jim Douglas.

Vermont was still a very Republican state in the early 1970s, so places like Middlebury College were critically important stops for Democratic candidates for statewide political office seeking any edge they could get. That desire—and the fact that WRMC-FM was popular throughout Addison County—meant that I had opportunities to meet, interview and report on many of the candidates in 1972 and 1974. That was heady stuff for a college student. Beyond making me feel more important, however, it provided me with a baptism of immersion into the real world of Vermont politics.

Much attention that political year was on the fierce fight for the Republican gubernatorial nomination featuring Attorney General Jim Jeffords and Luther "Fred" Hackett, a Burlington businessman favored by retiring Gov. Deane Davis. Not since the 1946 primary pitting Gov. Mortimer Proctor against Ernest Gibson, Jr., had there been such a bitter GOP gubernatorial fight. Jeffords, the progressive in the race, claimed "the Republican machine" was trying to ram through a victory for the more conservative Hackett. And it was.

Few people paid attention to Salmon's late-starting campaign. In a situation that is even more unbelievable given the early starts of campaigns today, Salmon only entered the race in late summer— because no one else would. He did so after returning fired up from July's Democratic National Convention in Miami, where he had been a McGovern delegate. Salmon's single previous statewide campaign, a 1970 race for attorney general against Jeffords, had been a disaster. And in 1972 being a McGovern delegate certainly wasn't an asset in Vermont. But everything fell Salmon's way. He was forty years old, a lawyer from Rockingham, handsome and charismatic in a Kennedy way. He came across as articulate, even though journalists would later mock his mangled syntax for giving us phrases such as, "Education is the fourth leg of the tripod of the state's economy" and, during the budget crisis of 1974, warning us that "Unless we seek to perform surgery on this patient now, like ships in the night, we'll be out of town." Most of all he struck a chord in the 1972 campaign with an anti-development theme and a compelling catchphrase that was unequivocal: "Vermont is not for sale." He called for a land speculation tax on the profits being made by developers and a program designed to ensure that Vermonters paid no more than a certain percentage of their income on property taxes.

Salmon was surely helped by the divisive GOP primary, won by Hackett, which upset liberal Republicans, who then either stayed home in November or backed Salmon. Hackett did not help his cause by seeming to give up the pro-environment position that Deane Davis had championed in office. Davis won passage in 1970 of Act 250, the state's pioneering development control law; Act 252, the state's unique pay-to-pollute water quality law; and the ban passed in 1972 on non-returnable bottles. But the leaders of the state GOP almost seemed to go out of their way in the 1972 campaign to trample on that environment-friendly image. The debate during those years produced one of the most famous lines in Vermont political history: Roland Seward, of Rutland, a top GOP leader, asked in a speech to the Springfield Rotary, "What are we saving the environment for? The animals?"

Just after the September primary, Hackett returned from a brief vacation to give a speech to the Society of Manufacturing Engineers, in which he withdrew his support for the bottle ban. In passing the ban, the 1972 Legislature had delayed implementation for one year, and Hackett, who favored recycling over returnable bottles and cans, said that "if the 1973 Legislature repealed that law, I would be in favor of it." Salmon used Seward's remark and Hackett's position on returnables to question the Republicans' general commitment to the environment. He had one line that always brought down the house. Speaking of the land speculators and developers who were gobbling up tracts of land in southern Vermont, he would yell out: "We're not going to change our laws! They're going to have to change their ways!"

When Salmon stopped by WRMC that September for an interview, I questioned him on a range of issues. What I remember more keenly than the interview, however, is what I said to him afterwards. I remarked as we walked out of the studio that it must be difficult going out every day to campaign knowing the odds were that you were going to lose. It was an impolite comment, but one that reflected the conventional wisdom. For many years I assumed and hoped Salmon had forgotten the remark, but in the 1980s I spoke before a management class he was teaching at the University of Vermont, and he recounted the exchange in introducing me.

Salmon went on to win in a victory that everyone labeled an upset, especially because it came as Republican Richard Nixon swept to re-election in a landslide. In fact, in Vermont, Republicans won all statewide contests except for governor. In an unusual analysis, outgoing Gov. Davis mused on election night that Hackett, as a Christian Scientist, had been too reluctant to attack Salmon, who was the first Catholic ever elected governor.

I am not sure what came first—my love of politics or of journalism—but I grew up in a house where we didn't eat dinner until Walter Cronkite had told us "That's the way it is." I was fascinated by the personalities in politics, and although I entered Middlebury College as a drama major, I soon switched to American history and brought the worlds of politics and journalism together in a senior thesis on John F. Kennedy and the press. Over my four years at Middlebury, I became increasingly involved with the college radio station, serving as station manager for two years and producing a number of radio shows reporting on the news in the state, including one that covered the 1972 campaigns that we called "Situation '72."

Jim Douglas won a seat in the state House in 1972. He campaigned hard, going door to door in the district, and used his broadcast skills to great advantage. He bought 30-second or 60-second ads in morning drive time on WFAD, the town's commercial AM station, and then stopped by the station to do the ad live. The morning announcer, Tim Buskey, feigning surprise, would say, "Look who's stopped by! It's Jim

Douglas! How are you this morning, Jim?" Then the two would chat informally for thirty or sixty seconds—and precisely at the end of the purchased time, Tim would quickly toss in, "The proceeding was a paid political announcement." I suspect few listeners ever caught on that the informal chats were campaign ads.

A few weeks before Election Day, Jim was involved in a minor car accident, which I seem to remember involved a logging truck. The local newspaper, *The Addison Independent*, ran a short item on the accident, listing the driver as James H. Douglas, of East Longmeadow, Massachusetts. Apparently, the person at the paper covering the police log didn't make the connection between the Jim Douglas involved in the fender bender and the Jim Douglas running for the state House—and neither did anyone else at the newspaper or in the campaign of Jim's opponent, Democrat Roy Newton. Jim had established residency in Middlebury and registered to vote in the town, but had not yet switched over his driver's license from the Massachusetts town where he had grown up, a fact that could have hurt his campaign by reminding voters that Jim was from out of state. I noticed the item in the paper and joked with Jim about it—and never once considered doing a story about it. That was the last time I buried the news. As my contacts expanded, I was quickly discovering how small a state Vermont is; I was beginning to realize that if I couldn't bring myself to report the news completely because I knew the subject of my story, I wouldn't make it very far as a journalist.

> I was quickly discovering how small a state Vermont is; I was beginning to realize that if I couldn't bring myself to report the news completely because I knew the subject of my story, I wouldn't make it very far as a journalist.

I covered Salmon's inauguration in January 1973 for WRMC, sending news reports and audio clips back to the station. It was my first visit to the State House as a journalist, albeit a college journalist, and my first since I had toured the building with my fellow eighth-grade Woodstock students. I remember little of Salmon's inauguration itself, but I do recall seeing the governor-elect a few hours prior to the ceremony. He was walking up the sidewalk next to the Pavilion Office Building, accompanied only by a state police trooper in plain clothes. He recognized me and stopped, and we talked for a few minutes. I could not get over the fact that the governor-elect was out walking — without a big entourage or heavy security — just before assuming the top job in the state. I would learn through the years how normal that is for governors of Vermont, who have no governor's mansion and who maintain their listed telephone number for their home residence.

The other big election while I was at the college was the 1974 race for the U.S. Senate. George Aiken was stepping down after 34 years in the Senate, and Republican Dick Mallary and Democrat Pat Leahy were vying for the seat. At the time I was still working at the college radio station, but I had also begun writing a political column for the *Valley Voice*, a new weekly Addison County newspaper whose publisher was John Michael White and whose editor was Gregory Dennis. They were eager to fill their pages, and so gladly signed me up to provide analysis of the campaigns, without any regard to my lack of credentials. In my first column I predicted that Mallary would win, a column that makes me wince as I look at it today. This race, following so closely on Salmon's unexpected victory, showed me before my professional career had even started that conventional wisdom was merely conventional and not always right. Twice burned, I never again made a prediction in print.

Leahy ran a masterful campaign and benefited from the Watergate backlash that hurt many Republicans that year. However, I wasn't alone in my handicapping; the *Rutland Herald* ran a headline on its front page the Friday before the election proclaiming, "CHITTENDEN POLL DOOMS LEAHY." The article reported on a poll taken by Vincent Naramore, a political science professor at St. Michael's College. On election night most news organizations were in Montpelier at the election center. By the luck of the assignment draw at WRMC, though, I was in South Burlington with Leahy as he became the first Democrat elected to the Senate from Vermont. The outcome was in doubt until after midnight, when Leahy told the crowd, "A funny thing happened on the way to the Naramore polls." Leahy delivered a great line that night. He said that when he started the campaign, he was told to prepare two speeches for election night: "one if you lose and one if you lose badly."

Following graduation from Middlebury in 1975 I married Nancy Price, a classmate who had been the editor of the Middlebury College newspaper, the *Campus*, an association that had led some on campus to accuse us of having a monopoly on the media. Two weeks later I went to work as the first fulltime news director of WFAD, the town's commercial radio station. This was a big step up from my previous part-time job at that station as host of a country western music show, something I knew nothing whatever about. My salary was $120 a week. The station's owners, Tim Buskey and Mark Brady, were starting up a new FM station at the same location and felt they needed to have someone covering the news for their expanded operations. I broadcast the morning and noontime news—my stepfather said in the beginning that I barked like a drill sergeant—and then went back to our apartment for a nap in the afternoon before heading out to cover a school board or selectmen's meeting in the evening. With only one car and with Nancy also working, I rode a bike to many of my interviews during the day, tie flapping in the wind and tape machine swinging from the handlebars. Town officials were sometimes abashed when I arrived on my bike at accidents or fires before the ambulance, police or fire vehicles. The station was very small, located for much of my time there in the back of a building on Court Street. The news teletype was in the bathroom—to quiet its noisy clacking and because there wasn't any other space for it. Every so often the bells would sound indicating a news bulletin, but I would often have to wait for someone using the facilities to finish up before I could rip the wire and see what had happened.

On Monday mornings I hosted a talk show that I started called "The Talk of Vermont." Sometimes, on the days when I had no guests but just took phone calls from listeners, I struggled to fill the hour. Once I rambled for quite a while waiting for the phones to ring. Finally a call came in, and I put it on the air only to have the listener ask if I had any idea whether it was okay to freeze "Chip and Dip." I had no idea, but I was so grateful to have a caller that I kept the woman on the phone for several minutes, suggesting possible places she could call to find out. Tim Buskey and I traded off hosting a Wednesday noontime talk show called "Lunch at Fire and Ice," an interview show that was broadcast live from a restaurant of that name. Tim did the softer interviews, and I interviewed the politicians. I loved the format and would have enjoyed hosting the show every week, but I knew that Tim loved the lunch as much or more than the interviews, and I wasn't going to cross the boss.

This was community radio at its best. One day I might be interviewing an elephant at a visiting circus; another day tape recording a story about the Addison County Fair and Field Days as I rode the Tilt-A-Whirl, my strained voice reflecting the twists and turns of the ride's spins. Whenever I made a mistake on the air—such as the time I mispronounced "nuclear" in a noon broadcast and then tried to fix it but repeated the wrong pronunciation four or five times like a broken record—I heard about it nonstop for days. The only time anyone ever offered me a bribe came a few months after I started working at the station fulltime. I reported on some problems at a local apple orchard, and the owner suggested that I feel free to come by the orchard at any time to pick up as many apples as I wanted.

Addison County is dairy country, and I quickly had to become an expert in all things dairy. I covered an outbreak of brucellosis— a highly contagious cattle disease—when it hit the state in the mid

1970s. At first I couldn't even pronounce the name of the disease, a real handicap when you're a broadcaster, so I wrote it phonetically in all my copy and still stumbled over it. The disease's return was being blamed on infected cattle brought in from out of state and led to the slaughter of many herds. My first big scoop was a story on how some Vermont dairymen were smuggling cows across state lines to circumvent regulations designed to stop the spread of the disease. The AP in Montpelier picked up the story and gave it good play. WFAD, not me, got credit for the story, but I couldn't have been prouder. Later I covered a meeting on brucellosis between farmers and U.S. Agriculture Secretary Bob Bergland, and later still went to Washington for a series of talk shows with USDA officials on dairy price supports.

More and more, though, Montpelier and the State House drew my attention. In 1974 Tom Salmon had easily won re-election as governor after an incredibly successful first term in office during which he delivered on his 1972 campaign promises to impose a tax on land speculators and provide property tax rebates to residents. But then came a recession. Unemployment soared and an energy crisis affected costs across the board. As Salmon put it many years later, "The tide ran out on us." In the fall of 1975, Salmon went on statewide television to call for a special session of the Legislature to raise the sales tax. This was a big deal: Vermont governors rarely go on television to make speeches. Moreover, only twenty times in Vermont's entire history had lawmakers been called into special session, and those sessions had dealt with the truly historic, like committing Vermont to the Civil War and responding to the 1927 flood. The most recent special session had been in 1966, when the newly reapportioned House met for the first time.

At WFAD we were part of the statewide network of radio stations that broadcast the governor's speech. After the speech I raced over to the Middlebury Inn to get reaction from the House Republican leader, Richard Snelling, who was in town speaking. Snelling declared without

34

hesitation that Salmon was wrong to call for the tax increase and wrong to call a special session. Moreover, he predicted that Salmon's proposal would quickly be defeated. No mincing of words there. This was my introduction to Snelling's overpowering presence. I was shocked that someone would defy the governor and vow, confidently, to defeat the governor's proposal. I headed to Montpelier to cover what would turn out to be a three-day special session that proved Snelling right. Lawmakers rejected Salmon's call to raise the sales tax. Snelling claimed the economy was rebounding fast enough to make higher taxes unnecessary, a stand history proved to be accurate and one that helped propel him into the governor's office in 1977.

> In 1974 Tom Salmon had easily won re-election as governor after an incredibly successful first term in office during which he delivered on his 1972 campaign promises to impose a tax on land speculators and provide property tax rebates to residents.

Salmon repeated his call for higher taxes when lawmakers reconvened in their regular session in January. Again he lost. A defeat in a U.S. Senate race in 1976 provided the final blow: Tom Salmon's career was over. No one told Salmon, though, and with the same irrepressible spirit that won him the governor's office, he built a law practice, helped to rescue Green Mountain Power Corp. from disaster when he took over as chairman, and then served as president of the University of Vermont, taking over at troubled times and helping to restore public trust in the institution. Ironically, but in a truly Vermont moment, Fred Hackett, the man Salmon defeated for governor in 1972, was the person who led the search committee that chose Salmon to head UVM.

I had the opportunity to watch Salmon's last year in office up close: In 1976, 1977 and 1978 I covered the legislative sessions for WFAD, spending three days a week in Montpelier and producing three reports a day that I phoned back to the station. When I started I had no idea what I was doing, I knew very few legislators, and I was intimidated by the other reporters, all of whom seemed to know and understand everything that was happening before it even occurred. That assignment, though, was pure fun: I wandered the halls of the State House, getting to know legislators, state officials and members of the press.

Legislative life was an informal affair then. Most lawmakers lived in Montpelier during the week and gathered in the evening to socialize, usually in the bars at the Brown Derby or the Little Valley House. Relationships existed then that would be frowned upon now. Reporters spent the evening drinking with lawmakers and even the governor—at least while Tom Salmon was still in office—and then covered those same legislators in the morning. Even during the day, however, many reporters played a role different from the one most of them do today, serving up a fair share of advocacy as part of their news coverage. Mavis Doyle was a legend and the best example of advocacy journalism. Her motto was to "afflict the comfortable, and comfort the afflicted." When she died in 1978 the Legislature said she had "consistently spoken for the needy and helpless in our society." Mostly she was known for doing whatever it took to get a story, whether it was listening at keyholes or going into the men's bathroom to hunt down a lawmaker. One story had her listening to closed-door deliberations of the Senate Judiciary Committee by hiding in the adjoining room with her ear glued to the crack around the connecting door. Unfortunately for her, her cigarette smoke seeped under the door and gave her away. I remember her for her constant ability to get under the skin of Dick Snelling, whom she often referred to in print as "the portly Shelburne industrialist."

Many lawmakers and their spouses passed the time in the card room, just off the House floor, playing bridge and cribbage; a few times each session an upright piano and fiddler set up shop, and Rep. Joseph Steventon, of Rochester, would lead the calls for square dancing. I made a concerted effort to get to know Bob Picher, who had been clerk of the House since 1963. He was the House's expert on rules, master of minutiae and keeper of the records. If I missed anything on the floor or didn't understand a parliamentary maneuver, Picher gladly filled me in. This guy loved his job and loved the House with a contagious enthusiasm. Picher was there when the House debated reapportionment and remembered Frank Hutchins crying on the House floor during the debate, mourning the passing of an era. "He was a tall skinny guy," Picher said as he pointed to Hutchins' seat at the time. He pointed again to another seat. "What's now seat 53; that's where Ethan Rule died, just after morning devotional in 1963." A pause. "Rule, of Waltham; he'd just married a younger woman," as if that explained everything. That reminded him of the day Sen. Asa Bloomer, R-Rutland, died, also at the State House. "He was such a dignified man. It was the seventh Thursday of the year, the day we were electing judges." The stories just rolled out, but, of course, he had plenty of material to work with.

One colorful character was Reid Lefevre, of Manchester, who wielded considerable influence over the affairs of state during the years he chaired the House Ways and Means Committee. Yet during the rest of the year he was better known as King Reid of King Reid's Shows, Vermont's only traveling carnival. One year he brought his carnival, complete with ponies and elephants, into the House chamber for a special performance. Another memorable legislator was John Boylan, a former railroad worker. He exerted almost complete control over the shape of the state's spending plan while he chaired the Senate Appropriations Committee. Jack O'Brien, a Chittenden County senator, was a professional fighter and sports promoter. Ernest "Stub" Earle, of Eden, kept a spittoon by his seat on the House floor to dispose of his chewing tobacco. John Murphy, who represented Ludlow in the House for thirty years, was credited with single-hand-edly keeping alive the labor movement in the state. He once said, "The people I represent will probably never visit the State House. In fact, the people that I represent probably don't understand in some cases there is a Vermont State House." And, of course, there was Sen. Gilbert Godnick, of Rutland, who so mangled the English language that we loved to get his reaction just to hear the latest "gillyism." Among his most famous: "We'll burn that bridge when we get to it" and "There's always one rotten egg in every bushel of apples." My favorite was "You three guys make quite a pair."

The Legislature then, as it is today, was a citizen Legislature, with the members spending their winters in Montpelier and going about their business back home the rest of the time. For some thirty years a State House window was left unlocked to allow the governor, lawmakers and members of the press to get back into the building at night. The not-so-secret entry was called the "Aiken Window," because it was first used in the 1930s by Gov. George Aiken, who liked to return to his office in the building at night but often forgot his keys. The window stayed unlocked throughout the 1960s, used primarily by members of the press who at that time had their offices up under the State House dome. Even today, individual Vermont legislators have no offices or staff.

> The bill was controversial, and at one point in the debate, Kunin sent [House Speaker Walter] Kennedy a note asking, "Do you think I should stop knocking my head against the wall?" Back came the reply: "Not until the calluses give you a problem with hats."

When I arrived in 1975 Timothy O'Connor was speaker of the House, the first Democrat ever to wield the gavel. O'Connor, from Brattleboro, was a moderate with conservative leanings liked equally by Republicans and Democrats. He had a bipartisan, easygoing nature and could have just as easily have been a Republican speaker as a Democratic one. It was telling that he won the office even though the Republicans held a 78-70 edge over Democrats. O'Connor followed Walter "Peanut" Kennedy as speaker, and it may be that House members wanted a little calm in the chair after Kennedy's more high-pressured style. I never saw Kennedy presiding, but in 1994 historian Howard Coffin invited me to a lunch he had arranged between Kennedy and then-Speaker Ralph Wright, a Democrat with a reputation for toughness that surpassed that of Kennedy's. Coffin had been a newspaper reporter in the 1970s, covering Kennedy, and was curious what would happen when these legends traded tales.

The conversation was fascinating. No matter what tale of muscle-flexing Wright boasted, Kennedy matched him—and then some. Wright had been accused of punishing his opponents by banishing them to unimportant committees; Kennedy did that. Wright had a run-in with Senate leaders when they pocketed a bill sent over from the House, delaying action; Kennedy recalled an angry confrontation when the Senate tried to steal a budget bill after it had been sent to the House. Kennedy stormed into the Senate chamber and grabbed back the bill. Kennedy, a car salesman from Chelsea, once said during a House debate, "I want you all to know I believe in honesty, even though I am both a politician and a car dealer."

Madeleine Kunin says that Kennedy helped her numerous times when she was a freshman legislator from Burlington, even though she was a Democrat. In her book, *Living a Political Life*, she tells the story of introducing a bill in 1973 that would have required lobbyists to disclose their expenditures. The bill was stuck in committee; its chairman, Henry Hicks, a friend of Kennedy's, wouldn't let it come to the floor. Kunin went to Kennedy, who told her "Well, this place needs a little shaking up." He suggested she try a little-used and rarely successful House rule that allows the full House to relieve a committee of a bill. Early the next morning, when many members still weren't in their seats or were busy reading up on that day's calendar, Kunin stood up and casually asked that the committee be relieved of H.492. Kennedy sounded bored as he asked for the ayes and nays, suggesting it was just a routine matter. The motion carried, and Hicks suddenly realized he had been had. The bill was controversial, and at one point in the debate,

Kunin sent Kennedy a note asking, "Do you think I should stop knocking my head against the wall?" Back came the reply: "Not until the calluses give you a problem with hats."

The bill failed, 64 in favor, 71 against. Kunin, a freshman legislator, was devastated. Then came this note from the speaker: "Madeleine. It was a whale of a try, and with the odds stacked against you, you fought an excellent and brave battle. You also gave many people cause to think. The news media will be kind to you, rough on your opponents. There will be another day and you will try again. Cheers. I have been beaten by experts myself. Sincerely, Pean."

Covering the Legislature for WFAD allowed me to work closely with the Montpelier bureau of the AP. The Associated Press is a cooperative relying heavily on its member newspapers and broadcast stations to provide stories from around the state. In 1975 the AP had only two people working in Vermont, so its resources were stretched pretty thin. To help them compensate, they gladly accepted all the help I was happy to provide. During the legislative sessions I phoned the bureau with breaking news or the outcomes of votes. And I began working for the bureau as a stringer on Sundays, the one day a week when the bureau was closed. I culled stories from newspapers and made checks with the police, and then wrote and dictated stories to the New Hampshire bureau, where a reporter fed them back on the Vermont wire.

John Reid was in charge of the Montpelier AP at the time. John is a native of Barre who went on to become a senior vice president of The Associated Press. We had gotten to know each other when he was working at the UVM radio station and I was at the Middlebury station. John lived out in Woodbury, a rural community twenty rough miles north of Montpelier, and sometimes had trouble getting to work— either because his pigs had gotten loose or his car had slid off the icy roads. So if I didn't see any Vermont news on the early morning wire I quickly picked up a few items from the morning papers and called the New Hampshire bureau to dictate several items—just to keep the broadcast wire fresh until John managed to dig out his car or corral the pigs. John worked hard to promote my work at WFAD within the AP, hoping to encourage me to apply for a job there. In January and April of 1978 he took two of my interviews with Dick Snelling and turned them into AP stories—giving me full credit. In July of that year he nominated me for a national award that at the time was given out by The Associated Press Broadcasters Association. Eager to work with him, I applied—but not successfully—when openings came up at the bureau. Even when the bureau expanded to three reporters, I was twice rejected. The reporters chosen—Nancy Shulins and Wayne Davis—went on to become exceptionally talented writers and editors at the AP, but I was too far removed from the process to see their potential personally. I only grew discouraged. I began to look at options in broadcast journalism. One possibility was working at a new television station in the Upper Valley, WNNE. Another opportunity I pursued was at Vermont Public Radio, which was just beginning to think about creating a news department. Finally, in the summer of 1978, I learned that the Vermont AP had another opening. John Reid had been named bureau chief in West Virginia. I wouldn't be working with him, but I resubmitted my application. The third time was the charm.

Jeff Danziger's editorial cartoon caricatures T. Garry Buckley and Dick Snelling.

"If I were going on a vacation I would have Snelling plan it, and then I would go with Garry."

—*State Rep.Emory Hebard*

Chapter 3

Learning the Ropes at the AP

MONTPELIER, Vt. (AP) – "It hurts too much to laugh and I am too old to cry," a subdued Lt. Gov. T. Garry Buckley said Wednesday of his defeat in the primary election.

Those words were the lede of the first bylined piece I wrote as a reporter for The Associated Press. The date was September 13, 1978, a Wednesday. I had started work two days earlier in the Montpelier bureau of the AP. On Tuesday, primary election day, I worked during the day for the AP but then returned to Middlebury to anchor WFAD's election night coverage—part of the deal the AP had worked out with WFAD to smooth over the fact that I was leaving the radio station. Generally, AP members don't look kindly on the AP poaching reporters they've trained. On Wednesday, though, I was back in Montpelier covering the Republican Party's unity luncheon. T. Garry Buckley, a Republican and the outgoing lieutenant governor after only a single two-year term, had lost to Peter Smith, founder and former president of the Community College of Vermont.

Buckley was a larger-than-life character whose swashbuckling style endeared him to reporters but rankled the GOP establishment. He and Gov. Richard Snelling clashed frequently during Buckley's time in office. Emory Hebard, a longtime state representative from Glover who later became state treasurer, privately summed up the differences between the two men this way: "If I were going on a vacation I would have Snelling plan it, and then I would go with Garry." Anytime we wanted a colorful quotation—and frank assessment—we sought out Buckley. He never disappointed. Buckley had launched his re-election campaign by flying a 1930s biplane—a Stearman—into Montpelier's Knapp Airport, hopping out of the plane wearing goggles and hat, and handing his nominating petitions to Reid Payne, the Legislature's sergeant at arms, who then delivered them to the secretary of state. Buckley's campaign posters that year showed him pulling on the prop of a replica of the Spirit of St. Louis, as if he were starting it. They carried his handwritten note: "Let's all pull for Vermont."

But the Republicans weren't sure Buckley was pulling with them, a sentiment that dated back sixteen years to the 1962 election, when Buckley and fellow Republican A. Luke Crispe threw their support behind the election of Democrat Phil Hoff as governor. The two had told the incumbent governor, Republican F. Ray Keyser, Jr., that if he chose an out-of-state buyer for the new Pownal horse-racing track, they would work for his defeat. He did and they did, and Keyser lost.

Buckley was a masterful politician who engineered one of the most amazing upsets in the state's history—an upset that also played into his 1978 primary defeat. Two years earlier Buckley had lost the popular vote in the 1976 race for lieutenant governor to John Alden, a Democrat from Woodstock. Alden received 82,632 votes—2,854 short of a majority—while Buckley received 81,471 and John Franco of the Liberty Union received 6,778. According to Vermont's

Constitution, in cases in which no candidate wins a majority, the Legislature, meeting in joint session, must hold an election. In modern times lawmakers have just rubberstamped the popular-vote winner, and candidates who lost the popular vote have not campaigned in the legislative vote. But Buckley did. He later said his phone bill for the month before the legislative election was $2,000. His feeling was that the Constitution clearly states that if no candidate wins a majority, there has been no election. "If the Constitution says there is no election, there is no election. It says the election shall be decided by the Legislature, and I took my case to them," he said years later.

The vote is by secret ballot so no one knows how anyone votes, but Buckley defeated Alden 90-87, with Franco receiving a single vote. At the time I was still working for WFAD and covering the State House. John Reid, of the AP, had covered the debate and then gone back to the AP bureau to prepare the news bulletin on the outcome. As the ballots were being counted, I called John on my phone in

> Buckley was a larger-than-life character whose swashbuckling style endeared him to reporters but rankled the GOP establishment. He and Gov. Richard Snelling clashed frequently during Buckley's time in office.

the House gallery to give him the results as soon as they were announced by the presiding officer, out-going Lt. Gov. Brian Burns. My headphones were hooked into the House sound system, and I heard the clerk telling Burns the results: "Buckley, 90..." I yelled into the phone that Alden had won. I had been thinking that with 180 members voting, the winner would need 91 votes, 50 percent plus one vote. But only 178 members voted, so 90 was the magic number—and Buckley had it. Luckily, John Reid was far more seasoned than I and waited patiently for the complete results to be announced before sending out his bulletin.

Buckley thus became the first state official since 1853 to win election by the Legislature after losing the popular vote. Most lawmakers did not disclose their votes—even to the media—but their comments showed the competing rationales. Some said they voted for the person they considered most qualified; some said they voted for Alden because he was the statewide winner of the popular vote; still others said they voted the way their legislative districts had gone. Some said privately they had voted for Buckley because they had heard that Alden was under criminal investigation, a fact not publicly known at the time but one that proved to be true. However, in 1978 Buckley paid a price for his earlier display of chutzpah. Smith's supporters argued during that year's primary campaign that if Buckley were the nominee he would face a backlash from voters who were upset he had usurped the will of the 1976 electorate.

Against that backdrop I attended the 1978 GOP unity luncheon and watched Buckley go out with class. Throughout the campaign he had confidently predicted he would defeat Smith by a margin of 60-40. "I had the percentages right," he ruefully told the Republican faithful at the luncheon. "It's just that the names were a little off." Then he provided me with the perfect quotation for ending my story: "I don't know what's going to happen to me. I'm too old to do anything else, but I'm too young to quit."

When the luncheon was over I raced back to the AP bureau, eager to write my story. I had a notebook of notes but no real idea what to do with them. Never before had I written a newspaper story. I had written my columns for the *Valley Voice*, but this was my first effort at crafting a news story. I could write excellent broadcast copy, but those stories ran fifty words. The AP's newspaper stories routinely ran 500 words or more—and I was lost. My new boss, Nancy Shulins, who became one of the AP's most talented writers, was a patient teacher, as was Wayne Davis, the other reporter in the small bureau. They worked long and hard over the next few months to turn my copy into coherent and at times colorful reports.

I quickly learned I had moved into a bigger league and that AP copy is carefully scrutinized by readers far and wide. I had attributed the quotation that led the story —"It hurts too much to laugh and I am too old to cry"— to Adlai Stevenson. Early the next morning, we received a call correcting my attribution. Stevenson had indeed spoken these words after one of his presidential defeats, but apparently he had borrowed them from Abraham Lincoln, who had used them after his 1858 defeat in a U.S. Senate race in Illinois.

As thrilled as I was with my new job at the AP, I was also intimidated, not just by what I didn't know about newspaper writing but by the fear that I might not live up to the faith John Reid had shown in recommending me over and over again. I was also acutely aware that I had just taken a huge step from a small-town broadcaster with a teletype in the bathroom to a print reporter whose stories might possibly be distributed across the entire country, even, perhaps, the world. This was a whole new game.

The New York Sun created The Associated Press in 1846, when its owner offered to share with his rivals news from the U.S. war with Mexico as the first step in building an alliance of newspapers. Another 110 years passed before the news cooperative opened a bureau in Vermont. In 1956 the AP finally sent Walter Mears, 21, five months out of Middlebury College, up from Boston to become its first correspondent in the state. Mears went on to be a legend in the AP, winning the 1977 Pulitzer Prize for his coverage of the 1976 presidential campaign. He remains a hero to me, and not only because we share a Middlebury education and both ran the Montpelier AP. He was meant for a larger stage, however. He was truly the best political writer the AP has ever had; he covered every presidential campaign from 1960 to 2000. Tim Crouse described the reporters on the 1972 presidential campaign in his book *The Boys on the Bus*, and wrote of how at the high-pressured news events the reporters would look to Mears and ask, "What's my lede, Walter?" Ironically, throughout my years as head of the Vermont AP bureau, Mears repeatedly told me that he envied me. Running the Vermont bureau was the best job he ever had, he still likes to say.

The AP's first office in Vermont was just a desk in what is called the Crow's Nest, one floor up from the Senate gallery next to the State House attic. In later years it moved to the basement of the old Tavern Motor Inn, but a flood in 1974 forced the AP across the street to the second floor of what's known as the Thrush Tavern building, an 1820s brick building at 107 State Street. The Thrush Tavern has been and remains a favorite watering hole for lawmakers and state officials. Countless stories for State House reporters have come from conversations with lunching legislators. Sometimes even a sighting of two warring lawmakers breaking bread together provided evidence of an important development.

I quickly learned I had moved into a bigger league and that AP copy is carefully scrutinized by readers far and wide.

The Thrush building stands next door to the Pavilion Office Building, built on the site of the old Pavilion Hotel. It is the main office building of state government. My office in the Thrush, on the second floor, in the back, was perfect for keeping an eye on state government. In the early 1980s the AP hung a small satellite dish outside one of the front windows of the office to draw down AP signals from satellites high above. Within a few days, an aide to Gov. Richard Snelling showed up at the door to check on the dish; the governor had seen it and feared its purpose was to eavesdrop on private conversations in his corner office. The dish did appear to be aimed at the governor's office, which was then located in the southeastern corner of the fifth floor of the Pavilion Office Building, which gives you a sense of how close we were to state government all those years. Next door, literally. Above a bar, really. We used to get a couple of calls every month from reporters in other AP bureaus who had noticed our address in the AP directory—second floor, The Thrush Tavern—and wondered if we were truly located above a bar. I never did much drinking there, but the often erratic hours I worked meant that I probably consumed enough Thrush burgers to last me a lifetime.

When I went to work there in 1978 the AP bureau consisted of two small rooms, both filled with clacking teletypes that printed out various AP wires at roughly sixty words a minute. Many mornings started with the chore of cleaning up a paper jam in one of the teletypes and changing the ribbon, which left my hands black with the ribbon ink for the rest of the day. I started wearing fewer white shirts. In the early 1980s we doubled the size of the bureau by taking over the other two rooms on the second floor. That's when I moved to an office at the rear of the building, a location that let me keep one eye on my work and one eye on the east wing of the State House, where Senate Finance and Senate Appropriations committees met. When the lights went out, I knew to run up and see whether the legislators had reached any agreement on a tax package. In 1986, though, the state built an addition onto the back of the Pavilion, moving the governor's office to a penthouse on the north end. That addition cost me my view of the State House and its golden dome, a view that had been a calming anchor for me as I went about my work.

Fortunately, I still had a view of the main parking lot of state government. I conducted many important interviews in that parking lot after I saw a top official arrive or prepare to depart. Those officials might duck my calls, but they couldn't escape the parking lot ambush. If I saw someone I needed to talk to walking to his or her car, I sprinted down the stairs, raced around to the back of the building, and waited at the bottom of the ramp, to the side of the parking lot, until they drove by. They had to stop. Top officials in the governor's office, Supreme Court justices and attorneys general all provided me with key information as the price to exit the parking lot.

Among the most dramatic events to hit our bureau in the thirty years above the Thrush Tavern was the March 1992 flood that forced us to evacuate the office. Early morning ice jams blocked the flows of the nearby Winooski River and its North Branch; within hours the downtown was underwater, and our building was surrounded by a sea. The streets to the office were all closed, so I hiked up into Hubbard Park, hitched a ride on the back of a city truck going through the park and walked—with my pant legs rolled up—into the Thrush building through a back kitchen door that Thrush owner Paul Rumley opened for me. The AP reporter who had opened the office that morning and I gathered some equipment and headed to the State House, where Speaker of the House Ralph Wright let us set up shop in his secretary's office. Later in the day our technician at the time, Tim Carver, and I persuaded a fish and game official with a Boston Whaler to bring us back to the building to get enough computer equipment to continue to operate from higher ground. We moved into a building on Baldwin Street, on the other side of the State House, that housed several news organizations and took over space once occupied by United Press International. We were back in our offices in about a week (The Thrush re-opened after six days for its traditional St. Patrick's Day bash), but the flood devastated many downtown buildings; some businesses never re-opened.

When I started with the AP, United Press International dominated the state, providing service to all but one newspaper. The AP-UPI rivalry, not just within the state, but globally, was the stuff of legend, full of battles between reporters for the two wire services who trumpeted as major victories postings that beat those of their rivals by even a minute. Every AP and UPI staffer could recite the wins and losses over major stories, as well as the lore, such as when UPI reporter Merriman Smith grabbed the radio telephone in the press car behind President Kennedy after the president was shot in Dallas, dictated his bulletin and refused to give up the phone to the AP reporter in the same car as the two wrestled for possession. Or how AP reporter Wes Gallagher had his wife keep a telephone line open outside the courtroom where twelve Nazi war criminals were on trial, giving the AP a one-minute beat on their convictions and death sentences. I was thrust into this competitive world within a month of joining the AP, and found myself up against a seasoned, gifted and highly competitive UPI reporter, Candy Page, now with *The Burlington Free Press.*

The story was of worldwide interest: A suspected West German terrorist had been caught sneaking across the border into Vermont. The resulting trial had the air of a circus, complete with one of the nation's most celebrated defense lawyers, William Kunstler, whose courtroom theatrics, alone, made the trial worth watching. Global attention had been guaranteed when William Webster, the director of the FBI, used a major Washington news conference to grandly announce Berster's arrest. And it heightened when the flamboyant Kunstler subpoenaed Webster, claiming that the FBI director had orchestrated the publicity over Berster's arrest to generate favorable publicity for the bureau and to call attention to the threat of terrorism. Kunstler, who led the defense team in the Chicago Seven trial, in which seven radicals were accused of conspiring to incite a riot at the 1968 Democratic National Convention, was a reporter's dream, providing a constant stream of colorful quotations. He loved seeing how far he could push the judge, Albert Coffrin, who was no-nonsense, conservative and very formal on the bench. One day Kunstler and his team returned late from lunch and Coffrin was steaming, but Kunstler went on at great length telling the judge what a delightful meal the defense team had enjoyed at Bove's Italian restaurant. It was just, he said, that the service was a little slow because the defense team was so large. Kunstler and his team also loved to play off against the prosecution team, led by U.S. Attorney William Gray and his assistants, Jerome O'Neill and Karen McAndrew.

Such an assignment should not have come to the new guy in the bureau, especially since I was completely inexperienced as both a newspaper writer and as a wire service reporter. But Nancy Shulins figured that because I was also too new to know how to handle the demands back in the AP bureau, it would be best for me to cover the trial while she and Wayne Davis held things together in the bureau and took charge of filing my dictated copy. Consequently, less than a month after going to work for the AP, I spent the month of October sitting in federal court in Burlington covering a high-profile trial that sent my byline around the globe. Arriving at the courthouse for the first day of jury draw, I could see this was a big event. Armed federal police were stationed on the roof of the courthouse and throughout the building. Berster, who was 28 and a small and seemingly shy, red-haired woman, walked into the courtroom surrounded by guards.

> For a young reporter fascinated by politicians and power, covering Snelling was like being invited to a seminar on the presidency taught by FDR and JFK.

The original FBI announcement of Berster's capture had termed her a suspected member of the West German Baader-Meinhof terrorist gang, but authorities later backed off and said they had no evidence of that. Gray presented the case more straightforwardly: Kristina Berster entered the country illegally. Kunstler countered that she had done so out of necessity, fleeing persecution in West Germany. Berster conceded in her testimony that she had carried a forged passport as she walked across the border in Alburgh, but she claimed she did so to find sanctuary in the United States. "My intent," she said in her defense, "was to find refuge in the United States, to start a new life...to come out of this life of being persecuted and on the run....This country has a long tradition of welcoming refugees. It is even written on the national monument—the Statue of Liberty."

The case went to the jury in the last week of October, and I kept an eye on the calendar because my wife and I had made arrangements to move from Middlebury to Montpelier on Saturday, the 29th. For five days the jury deliberated before returning a guilty verdict Friday night on five counts of violating passport laws. When the congregation of reporters covering the trial heard the jury was returning with a verdict, I flew down a flight of stairs to a pay telephone and called the AP bureau, left the line open and the phone dangling, and went back to the courtroom. After the verdict was announced, I ran to the phone. I don't know if my story beat Candy's onto the wire, but I felt inaugurated into the competition of wire service reporting.

Back in Montpelier I picked up the assignments of covering the governor, politics and the Legislature. I covered other news, as well—the courts and Vermont Yankee were also regular assignments in those early years— but I spent most of my time covering Dick Snelling, a Republican then in his second year in office. For a young reporter fascinated by politicians and power, covering Snelling was like being invited to a seminar on the presidency taught by FDR and JFK. Everyone who met Snelling—friend or foe (and there weren't many in between)—felt the strength of his overpowering personality, how he commanded whatever stage he was on and his self confidence, which critics considered arrogance and which often manifested itself as impatience with others. I was also struck by his assumption, which seemed naïve in a politician, that logic and reason guarantee success. What I admired most, though, was his strong belief that leaders should lead, without regard to how controversial their decisions may be. "My prejudice about politicians is that they discover what would please the people," he told me once. "They also discover what is controversial— and therefore dangerous—and avoid it."

Snelling's strong belief in doing what he thought was right made him unpredictable. He defied conventional labels of liberal or conservative starting right after his election in 1976, when he named Sister Elizabeth Candon, a highly respected Democrat who had worked for Snelling's opponent, as his secretary of human services. In 1977, despite his reputation as a friend of business, he fired off biting criticism of the Vermont Yankee Nuclear Power Corp., saying, "If the technical competency of Vermont Yankee was as bad as its public relations, we'd all be in the dark." He vetoed popular legislation to help the financially ailing Green Mountain Race Track, in Pownal, saying, "We can't give in to this incessant blackmail." In 1979 he stood up to members of his own party in the Legislature who were promoting a no-growth budget, telling them that "a government which panders to the immediate demands of the public for superficial solutions can only continue to erode the public confidence on which it rests." He twice vetoed legislation to raise the drinking age, fired the commissioner of public safety, took on an anti-poverty agency he felt was misusing funds (the head of that agency referred to Snelling as the "porky flatlander"), created and financed a New Deal-type public works jobs program when times were tough, fought the state's utilities to forge an agreement with Quebec to purchase hydro-electric power, and okayed the controversial dawn raid of the Northeast Kingdom Community Church to determine if sect children were being abused.

Cornelius Hogan, who was Snelling's commissioner of corrections, tells of a family vacation he took in 1977 at a beach cottage in New Jersey. Snelling called Hogan's office early one morning and, says Hogan, "my wonderful deputy at the time, Martin Fitzgerald, then uttered the fateful words, 'He can't be reached.' One half hour later, a New Jersey state trooper was knocking at my door. [Snelling] was tough, and some people couldn't take that. However, those that stuck with him and learned from him were provided with gifts that last a lifetime."

Covering the Snelling administration was fascinating, but it was also a chore because Dick Snelling did not like the press. He felt reporters were lazy and too interested in covering conflict rather than understanding policy. We in the press considered him to be overly sensitive to what was written about him, but in a speech to the Vermont

Press Association in 1977 he spelled out why he was so sensitive. "I would beg you to understand that for most of us in public life, we are what you say or picture us as being," he said. A year later in a meeting with the editorial board of *The Burlington Free Press*, Snelling let his frustrations tumble out: "When I am through with this job, I'm going to start a backfire that will make you sit up and take notice," he said as he detailed his dream of creating a foundation to keep an eye on the press once he left office. "It would be nice if the person who gets misquoted doesn't have to get down on his hands and knees" [to win a retraction], he said.

In March 1980 I became the head of the AP bureau in Montpelier, which meant for five years I was the person whom Snelling called and wrote with his criticisms of AP stories. There were many, aimed at all of the reporters in the office. But his scrutiny made us better reporters. He started tape recording his news conferences and interviews to ensure that he was not misquoted. That prompted us to do the same. Time and again I was glad I had done so because I found in listening to the tape back in the bureau that I had missed a crucial comment in my notebook. He also forced us to take a closer look at some of the language we used. In 1979, for example, I wrote an analysis detailing how Snelling's proposal for a 6-percent growth in state spending was opposed by 59 of the 81 House Republicans, including the chairmen of the Appropriations and Ways and Means committees, the Republican leader and assistant leader, all of whom were on record opposing any increase in spending. I concluded that Snelling would have to rely on Democrats such as Lt. Gov. Madeleine Kunin, and noted that "Mrs. Kunin was the subject of dozens of verbal assaults from Snelling during the last session of the Legislature." I am sure I gave no thought to the use of the words "verbal assaults" beyond jazzing up my copy.

The day the story ran, however, Snelling shot me a two-page letter complaining that I had done an injustice to the political process.

He wrote, "There really is an enormous difference between disagreeing on a policy proposition and a 'verbal assault.' Decent people do not assault each other verbally or otherwise, and I will be surprised if you can show me even one 'verbal assault' which I made on Mrs. Kunin when she served as chairman of the House Appropriations Committee. I am constantly running into this problem, and the damage I think it does is to generally degrade the political process. The public gets a picture of public officials snarling at each other like cats and dogs."

Many of my colleagues were angry and defensive when they received such letters or calls from Snelling. I was not, choosing instead to learn from them. Whenever I speak to groups—of politicians or reporters—about covering politics and elected officials, I mention Snelling's 1977 comment to the press association that "for most of us in public life, we are what you say." I also tried to keep his comments in mind in future years when other politicians came calling with their criticisms.

Snelling's letters never stopped. In one that he wrote to me in 1983, he called me "the most competent, objective and professional newsman I know." But he just couldn't resist. In classic Snelling style he went on to say that he wasn't complaining about a column of mine that had run in the previous Sunday's *Rutland Herald*, but he did manage to fill two pages with criticisms of what I'd written and how I'd written it. In 1999 I was on hand when the state archives unsealed Snelling's private papers from the eight months he served as governor in 1991. Among the boxes of documents was a memo to his executive assistant that said, "Quite some time ago, it was agreed that we were going to set up a special meeting with Chris Graff—sort of a deep background meeting. Time goes on and he continues to write things that bother me and do not seem to be factually correct."

There's an old saw in reporting that as long as you spell a subject's name correctly, you can pretty much say whatever you want about him or her. But I did not find that to be true. In my thirty years of reporting, I found that people complained all the time, regardless of how I spelled their names. Snelling was on the right track, though, in thinking that more shared information helped us write better stories. I learned over time that most issues involve many shades of gray, but that hue remains hidden if the politicians only paint them in black and white.

Madeleine May Kunin served as governor of Vermont from 1985 to 1991.

"You have to approach the job with a sense of excitement and a sense that change is possible."

— Gov. Madeleine Kunin

Chapter 4

The Amazing Journey of Madeleine Kunin

Madeleine May Kunin swept into the House chamber, wearing white and radiating happiness. Wave after wave of applause and cheers accompanied her arrival as a small chamber group played Handel's "Water Music." This was a most historic moment, and every person in the chamber knew it. The air seemed electrified. One woman rode a bus all the way from Detroit just to be on hand when Vermont's first woman governor assumed office. Kunin's inauguration fell on January 10, 1985, and I stood at the curtain behind the speaker's podium, watching her triumphal walk down the chamber's center aisle. Her brother Edgar, a state senator, led the delegation of state representatives and senators escorting her to the podium where she would take the oath of office.

Kunin's inauguration came 45 years after she, then six, Edgar, then ten, and their mother arrived in this country aboard the *SS Manhattan*. Her family was Jewish, and had lived in Germany and Switzerland, before returning first to Germany and then to Switzerland. In 1936 their father had committed suicide, leaving their mother to face alone the prospect of rearing their children under the growing threat from Hitler. Now, in 1940, on the eve of the United States' entry into World War II, they were emigrants again, completing a journey begun two weeks earlier when they climbed aboard a train in Zurich, Switzerland.

Steaming up toward the Statue of Liberty, Kunin and her brother knew only three words of English, but they were fortified by their mother's belief in the "limitless dream of what this country could offer her and her children." Madeleine and Edgar certainly didn't disappoint her. Edgar went on to win a Pulitzer Prize in journalism, serve in the U.S. government and become a Vermont state representative and state senator. Madeleine also became a journalist and then entered politics. In her 1994 autobiography, *A Political Life*, Kunin thanks her mother for instilling in her many of the qualities that made her successful in life and in politics: ambition, perseverance, optimism and tolerance.

Madeleine Kunin's amazing ride did not end with her six years as governor. She became a close ally of Bill Clinton in his 1992 race for president, was one of three people who led his search for a vice presidential nominee and served on his transition team after his victory. Clinton named her deputy secretary of education, and then in 1996 he nominated her to serve as U.S. ambassador to Switzerland. The symbolism of the nomination was inescapable. Clinton was asking her to represent her adopted country in her native land; to reside in a country her mother had fled; and to return as a representative of the president of the United States, where her mother had dreamed that anything is possible. I flew to Washington to attend Kunin's swearing in as ambassador in the ornate Benjamin Franklin State Dining Room atop the State Department. Madeleine Albright, then the ambassador to the United Nations, administered the oath. She caught the emotion of the moment, saying, "For Madeleine Kunin today marks both the beginning of a new journey and a return to a place called home. America has always been made stronger by the survivors, by those who understand the value of freedom because the experience of their own lives forbids them from taking the blessings of freedom for granted. So it has been with Madeleine May Kunin."

It was a long journey from Ellis Island to the roof of the State Department but what started as activism fell into politics as if the route were greased. She came to Vermont in 1957 to write for *The Burlington Free Press*. She was following Edgar May into journalism; he had worked for a weekly newspaper in Bellows Falls before heading to the *Buffalo Evening News*, where he won the Pulitzer Prize in 1961. Four children later, as her eldest child headed off to kindergarten in 1966, Kunin began campaigning to have sidewalks built on her street so children could safely walk to school. Defeated in that effort, she lobbied successfully several years later, from a different house, to have red flashing lights installed at the railroad tracks her children had to cross to attend school. A sense of empowerment from that victory led her to run for the state House in 1972. She won that election and served three terms in the House. In her third term, Speaker Timothy O'Connor appointed her to chair the House Appropriations Committee, the all-important committee responsible for the state budget. She assumed control of the panel in 1977, just as Republican Richard Snelling took office as governor, leading to some lively exchanges between the two. Often I was the messenger between them, seeking a response from Kunin, for example, when Snelling declared her committee's proposed state budget irresponsible. She couldn't believe he felt that way because, from her perspective, the committee's budget was very much in line with the one Snelling proposed. To convince her, I had to play the tape of my interview with the governor, and I think this was one of the first times she realized that she was now on the front lines of political battle.

In 1978 Kunin ran for lieutenant governor expecting to face the incumbent, T. Garry Buckley, in the November election. However,

Buckley lost to Peter Smith in the September primary. This set up a match that appeared to favor Smith, who had won considerable favorable press for his upset win over Buckley. Although the governor and lieutenant governor are elected independently in Vermont, Smith seemed to be getting a boost from Snelling's popularity as he sought re-election as governor. Late in the campaign, though, Smith ran into rough publicity when a reporter asked him about the impact of running against a woman. "Oh, all the broads will vote for Madeleine," he replied blithely, hardly even wincing as the bullet went through his foot. His response sparked a fiery backlash. Buttons and T-shirts proclaiming "Broads for Madeleine" showed up around the state, and Kunin won the office.

"Being a caretaker is not my job description for the governor of the state of Vermont," Kunin declared. "The next governor should offer new ideas and new initiatives."

Four years later, she launched a campaign for governor after Snelling announced his retirement. She was instantly the frontrunner, but then an editorial appeared in *The Burlington Free Press* urging Snelling to run again. The editorial led to a petition drive that eventually persuaded Snelling to seek a fourth term. As quickly as Kunin had become the frontrunner, she now became the underdog. Although utterly discouraged in the face of Snelling's record and imposing persona, she did not back down. She couldn't. All the driving qualities she had inherited from her mother prevented her from quitting and disappointing the people who believed in her. In the coming months, however, crowds of supporters and the encouraging words she heard on the campaign trail buoyed her. She began to think that victory was possible. In her autobiography Kunin writes that the loss, when it came in November, was incredibly hard for her: "I truly had believed I would win. I have made a fool of myself."

In January of 1984 Snelling announced he would not seek re-election—and this time he meant it. Kunin put aside the hurt of the 1982 defeat and entered the campaign. Like her mother before her, she felt she had to be a role model for her children. She wanted them to see her as someone unafraid to try again. She also felt an obligation to the Vermonters who had supported her first run, even in the face of discouraging odds, and perhaps most importantly, she felt obliged to make this effort to move on with her life. "I had to exorcise the loss," she wrote in her autobiography. "It had to be removed surgically and be replaced with victory. That was how, at last, I would heal."

Her opponent this time was John Easton, the attorney general. He was handsome and appealing, with a strong record as a consumer advocate. Early in the campaign he developed an attention-grabbing campaign gimmick called "Working with Vermonters," whereby he spent one day a week working a blue-collar job. Photos abounded of Easton at a construction site or in a factory or, in one shot by the AP's Toby Talbot reprinted around the state, wearing a hard hat and work shirt while belted to a utility pole he was climbing in Stockbridge. Polls conducted just after the September primary showed Easton ahead of Kunin, helped in part by his primary win over retired banker Hilton Wick. But then Easton told a reporter that with the state's fiscal woes the next governor would be restricted from implementing many new initiatives. The new governor would have little choice but to "be a caretaker," he said. Kunin pounced on the phrase and firmly planted the label on Easton. "Being a caretaker is not my job description for the governor of the state of Vermont," she declared. "The next governor should offer new ideas and new initiatives. You have to approach the job with a sense of excitement and a sense that change is possible."

That election night was one of the longest I ever experienced. At the time the AP and United Press International had joint responsibility for organizing and running the Vermont Election Center, which tabulated votes in the statewide races. The election night tally is unofficial, but news organizations use it to determine winners and losers. In 1984 the election center was located in a building behind the Tavern Motor

Inn, in Montpelier. Back then a team from a local business supply store, Capitol Stationers, brought adding machines to provide the cumulative count. Far from high tech, overhead projections flashed town results on screens. Campaign workers and the curious lined up behind a security rope to watch the tally; excitement filled the air as the returns poured in and leads changed. The business supply store employees handed us printouts of the town and cumulative returns—and it was my job to declare the unofficial winner for the AP, while, at the time, Rod Clarke had the same responsibility for UPI. That night, in the governor's race, the lead switched several times. At one point Kunin led by a single vote. Just before 11 p.m. Kunin led, but Easton took the lead a few minutes later. Easton led through the early morning hours, but then Kunin edged ahead again. It was too close for me to make a call—the AP has always preferred accuracy to speed in its reporters—but Rod declared Kunin the winner sometime after 3 a.m. He was right, but it was as close as they come: Kunin, 116,938; Easton 113,264.

K unin had a difficult relationship with the press. The irony of this did not escape those of us who knew she had worked for WCAX and *The Burlington Free Press* and knew her way around the business. Part of the problem stemmed from her shyness. When she first ran for lieutenant governor she was uncomfortable campaigning. I remember being with her at a dinner event at the Middlebury Inn in 1978 as she watched Peter Smith rise and start working the room. She eyed him as he went from table to table, and finally she said—unhappily—that she guessed she had better make the rounds, too. Acute sensitivity to criticism also plagued her. More than once the governor's aides told me that a story I had written had provoked a gubernatorial migraine.

At the heart of the tension was her belief that journalists did not understand a woman's style of campaigning and governing. Her feeling on the subject was so emphatic that sometimes we in the press were made to feel that we were covering a governor not of a different gender but of a different species altogether. She repeatedly accused me of having no idea how to cover a woman. This was especially true when she ran against Snelling in 1982 and then after she replaced Snelling as governor in 1985. Kunin felt that the press was so accustomed to Snelling's strong-arm style that we did not appreciate her consensus style. In fairness to her, she was in a difficult spot. Anyone who followed Snelling into the governor's office faced fierce comparisons because of his overpowering personality, but I thought at the time that Kunin too quickly dismissed all criticisms as being driven by gender bias. She was right that we had no experience covering a woman governor, but we were much more interested in covering her style and her policies than her femininity. My feeling was that different women have different styles, just as men's styles can differ, and the press would roll with whatever came along. Tom Salmon and Dick Snelling were both men and about as different as can be in their management styles, and yet we had covered them and adjusted to them.

We in the press had to get along with Kunin to some extent. The relationship between reporters and the public officials they cover is necessarily symbiotic. Neither can exist without the other, and this results in a constant give and take. My children were still young during Kunin's terms, but every night at dinner they got a regular dose of Vermont news, consuming it like a sixth food group. At the time, I think they thought all their friends had two writers for parents and that governors called their friends' houses in the evenings and on Saturday mornings to chew out their fathers just as governors called their own house. One day my son, Garrett, then in third grade, announced that he wanted to interview Kunin for his class newspaper. He knew that I wrote about the governor regularly, and I am sure it never occurred to him that eight-year-old boys might not have the same access to the state's highest public official. Kunin, though, knew that a little kindness couldn't hurt, and she graciously agreed to the interview. We have a photograph from that meeting: Garrett and the governor sitting on the couch in her office, the golden dome of the State House looming large in the picture window behind them. Kunin is leaning attentively forward to speak directly into the fat microphone on my son's Fisher-Price tape recorder. Garrett is a journalist himself now in Washington, D.C., but that story in the class's photocopied newspaper was his first bylined interview with a public official.

In her autobiography Kunin confessed that "It was my deepest fear to be regarded as a weak woman." She also wrote of how hard it was for voters to accept her style of governing and how upset she was when Peter Freyne, a columnist for a weekly newspaper who later briefly served as her press secretary, dubbed her "Straddling Madeleine."

Kunin's style of governing made her vulnerable to criticism, just as Snelling's had made him an easy target. She was thoughtful in answering questions, sometimes to the point of seeming equivocal. She was soft-spoken, controlled and polite, in contrast to her predecessor's bombastic personality. She did not want to be just a governor; she was determined to be a woman governor, and she intentionally brought to the office stereotypical feminine qualities of accommodation, a desire to please and non-confrontation that sometimes worked for her and sometimes against.

However, Kunin was certainly right in one respect. A woman governor was a novelty in 1985. More than once Jim Dimmick, head of Kunin's state police security detail, was mistakenly identified as the governor at out-of-state meetings. Kunin says a woman handing out credentials at her first meeting of the National Governors Association gave the governor's name tag to her husband, Arthur, and she remembers many meetings of governors at which speakers addressed the assembly as "gentlemen."

The year Kunin became governor was a big one for us at the AP. Part of my job was to market the AP within Vermont, and when I took over the Montpelier bureau in 1980 the AP served only about half of the broadcast stations in the state and a single newspaper. By 1985, however, we had signed on all of the state's newspapers, radio and television stations, making Vermont the first state in the nation where the AP had 100 percent of the business. My boss at the time, based in Concord, New Hampshire, was Jon Kellogg, an outgoing person highly respected by editors around the region. (In 2004, now an editor at a newspaper in Connecticut, he received the Yankee Quill Award, the highest honor given by New England journalists.)

Together Jon and I had tramped around the state visiting newspapers to trumpet AP accomplishments and show off our photos and stories. Some editors conceded we did good work. But they worried about the transient nature of the AP, where great reporters like John Reid, Nancy Shulins and Wayne Davis moved on to other assignments in the AP within a year or so of taking over the Montpelier bureau. They wondered who would be there in the coming years. I assured them I planned on staying. In 1983 the AP had asked me to be the bureau chief in Nashville, the first of several promotion offers that came my way, but I enjoyed the uniqueness of the Montpelier job, which allowed me to run a bureau while still writing and reporting.

> Once in an interview with a newspaper reporter [Speaker Ralph] Wright dismissed something I had written with the comment, "Ah, Graff, he's just a Republican."

As we were picking up more and more business in Vermont, UPI was running into financial problems. The news service abruptly decided to all but pull out of Vermont, suddenly cutting its staff from three to one and overnight dropping its Vermont-filed news for broadcast stations. It did so without telling its clients. Consequently, news broadcasters such as Steve Zind, who was then with WNCS in Montpelier, showed up for work on Thursday, May 16, 1985, to find no Vermont news on the UPI wire.

At the time my friend John Reid was in charge of the AP broadcast division, based in Washington. Before UPI had a chance to reconsider its decision to pull out of Vermont, John air freighted up to Vermont a dozen high-speed printers and satellite dishes for stations to receive AP news. He also sent up a team of technicians from New Jersey to install the equipment. Our broadcast salesman from Boston, Daryl Staehle, went from station to station, persuading the owners to sign AP contracts. By Saturday nine of the thirteen stations that had been UPI clients were receiving AP news. The remaining stations would follow, as would three of the state's daily newspapers still receiving UPI. Norman Runnion, at the time the managing editor of the *Brattleboro Reformer* and a former UPI foreign correspondent, said of his old employer, "I have rarely observed such irresponsible and cowardly behavior with anybody I have encountered in the news business." In order to ensure that we would be able to meet responsibilities while serving the new members, the AP added more staff to the Vermont bureau. A fourth reporter had been added in 1981, and now a fifth was added, in 1986, with a staff photographer to come in 1987.

Kunin's first year in office was pretty rough. Her appointees had trouble adjusting to their posts, she had poor relations with the Legislature and many of her major legislative initiatives failed. Kunin herself came across in her first year as extremely cautious. Her tendency was to study matters and issues carefully, even to the point of second-guessing her appointees. But the biggest obstacles in her first year were members of her own party. In 1985 Democrats won the office of speaker of the House and took control of the Senate; a Democrat, Sen. Peter Welch, became the first person of his party ever to hold the position of president pro tem of the Senate. Everything should have been golden for Kunin. However, some of the Democrats were feeling their oats with their newfound powers and some simply felt Kunin was too conservative.

Surprisingly, or maybe not, one of her harshest critics was Sen. Phil Hoff, who grumbled at one point that Kunin sounded more like a

Republican than a Democrat. Hoff, the firebrand governor of the 1960s, had dropped out of elective politics after losing his 1970 bid for the U.S. Senate, but in 1982 he decided to re-enter the fray and won a seat from Chittenden County in the state Senate. He served six years and found the whole process frustrating. He made it clear that he had been much happier when he was the chief executive. With Kunin replacing Snelling in 1985 and the Democrats in charge of both the House and Senate, Hoff felt the party had a unique opportunity to push through a reform agenda, and he was disappointed when the one he had in mind failed.

The cold shoulder Kunin received in the Senate was in sharp contrast to the support she won in the House. Credit for that fell to Ralph Wright, of Bennington, who will beat out Peanut Kennedy in the history books in the contest over who was the most powerful speaker in the history of the state. Wright won election as speaker in 1985, despite the fact that Republicans outnumbered Democrats 78-72. The state had never seen anything like him before, and it may never again. Wright looked and acted as if he had stepped out of central casting and was playing the part of speaker of the Massachusetts House in the days brought to life in Edwin O'Connor's *The Last Hurrah*. The silver-haired Wright was originally from Massachusetts, an Irish-Catholic whose passion for the little guy was palpable, with an us-versus-them mentality that reflected the Marine he had been. He rarely spoke; he growled. "Graff," he would snarl. "You're up to no good." We in the press made no effort to protect him from himself; we presented him as he was: a caricature of a caricature. But no one could deny how well he worked the House.

Once in an interview with a newspaper reporter Wright dismissed something I had written with the comment, "Ah, Graff, he's just a Republican." I responded with a letter detailing that I had gone to great pains over the years to be nonpartisan. I didn't expect a response but Wright graciously wrote a letter to the editor of the publication in

which his interview appeared, saying he had no basis for his character-
ization and felt that I was a fair reporter.

Many people, mostly Republicans, thought Wright rose every
morning wondering who he would crush or punish or defeat that day.
I didn't see him that way. I thought he woke every day wondering what
he could do to make the world a better place. I think that's why he and
I got along so well; we had both been around long enough to be cynics,
but neither of us was. We both remained awed by the State House and
by governors. Wright came across as merciless, but that didn't fit the
picture of him talking to school children or visitors when you could hear
the reverence for democracy in his voice. Not many felt as I did, and
over his ten years as speaker critics called him ruthless and tough and
dirty. Part of the reason I admired him, though, was that he used the
powers of his office to get what he wanted. Yes, his style was different
from anything ever before seen in Vermont, but I gave him credit for
seizing the opportunity to accomplish the work he wanted to do.

Among his many talents, Wright had an uncanny ability to count
to 76—the number of votes needed to pass a bill. "Any first grader can
get to 76, but it takes a doctorate in politics to know where to go to
get the 76," wrote Wright in his autobiography. "I never, ever, literally
twisted anyone's arm. Did I ever do what amounts to the same? You bet
your life I did. I used all the cunning and charm I possessed to win.
Sometimes it wasn't enough, but more often than not it did the job."

Wright played counterpoint to Kunin's non-confrontational style,
and was a blessing when it came to moving along her goals. He and his
Democratic leader, Paul Poirier, saved her agenda time and again,
although the duo fought Kunin once over property tax relief—and
they won. Nonetheless, Kunin relied on Wright to help push through
her major education financing reform package in 1987, as well as some
of the major environmental initiatives that were the hallmark of her
tenure. The keystone of those initiatives was a planning law that became
known as Act 200.

Once again a commission had been formed and galvanized around the fear that development was running rampant in Vermont. It was the same fear that had prompted Gov. Deane Davis to develop and pass Act 250 in 1970 and Gov. Tom Salmon to impose taxes on land speculation in 1973. What made the concerns of 1987 different, though, was the question of who would control that growth. Kunin devoted most of her 1988 state of the state address to the issue, saying, "Our task is to shape the Vermont of tomorrow." Her proposals detailed guidelines for growth. The law finally enacted by the 1988 Legislature contained 32 principles for planning that were streamlined in 1990 into a dozen goals. Property rights advocates fought Kunin, protesting that she was undermining local control, but she countered that the law gave the public a say in how development happened. Act 200, she said, "is how you keep the vision of Vermont. Act 200 symbolizes a sense of community and working together for the future of the state."

As 1990 opened Kunin pondered a possible bid for a fourth term. She knew that polls showed her popularity had fallen and that she would face a tough fight against Richard Snelling, who had decided to try to regain the office of governor because of his fears over the state's fiscal health. Kunin announced in April that she would not run, but when I had interviewed her a month before that announcement, she said that she was confident she could win; she just did not feel a compelling need to prove it.

"Whatever I decide, I will not decide out of bitterness or anger," she said. "I don't have to run again to prove a point. I have proven I can do the job. History is not going to record whether it is three terms or four terms, nor do I have to run to prove I am not afraid. On one level it is a very personal decision, but it is more than that. You don't do this for yourself. You do this hoping to do some good."

Chris Graff at a 1980s press conference with then Gov. Dick Snelling.

"Making government productive, making it work, that's not the stuff of which heroes are made."

— *Gov. Richard Snelling*

Chapter 5

A Changing of the Guard: Snelling and Dean

A t the State House, workers had draped bunting from every column and cornice until the building resembled a colorful wedding cake. No one cared if the red, white and blue decorations were extravagant. For days tourists and Vermonters alike had been lining up on the sidewalk leading up to the state capitol to have their photographs taken for posterity in front of the festooned building. The occasion was Saturday's celebration of Vermont's bicentenary.

On the fifth floor of the nearby Pavilion Office Building, the governor's staff worked out details of the upcoming meeting of the National Governors Association in Seattle. At Wesson's Family Restaurant, in South Burlington, the governor's press secretary waited for the governor to arrive for a breakfast meeting.

It was early morning, August 14, 1991, and no one knew yet that Gov. Snelling had died.

Marselis Parsons, news director of WCAX-TV, provided me with the first word of the governor's death. One of his reporters had heard a scanner call that an ambulance was headed to the Snelling home in Shelburne. Parsons, who also lives in Shelburne, drove to the governor's home. He pieced together the story, and called me to help get confirmation, which came quickly.

At approximately 8 o'clock two state police troopers had discovered Richard Snelling's body in the backyard by the pool. Half an hour later Lt. Gov. Howard Dean, who was giving a physical exam to a patient at his Shelburne medical practice, learned he was now the governor of the state of Vermont.

And so began coverage of one of the biggest stories in the state's history. I sat down and began to write, operating almost on autopilot. I wrote the story on Snelling's death, updating it more than a dozen times, wrote a more complete obituary and then added a news analysis about this most complex person. I went up to the State House to attend Dean's swearing-in in the afternoon, and then again late in the day. I was emotionally spent, and I went to the place where I would feel most acutely the loss of a man who was so much larger than life. I didn't go to be consoled, but to remember.

The information came surprisingly quickly that morning, but for every question answered there were two new ones.

We learned that Snelling likely died of a heart attack the previous night; that his widow, Barbara, was on business in New York state; that Dean automatically became governor upon Snelling's death. From the state archives came word that Snelling was the first governor to die in office since Gov. Peter Washburn in 1870; we then learned that New York police had located Mrs. Snelling, and she was flying back to Vermont aboard a New York state airplane.

Dean arrived at the governor's office shortly after noon. The chief justice officially swore him in around three o'clock. I have never forgotten how odd that moment was: Everyone in that room was mourning Snelling's death. Dean, although mindful of the death that had put him in these circumstances, grinned in spite of himself after he was sworn in. This was a personal moment of celebration for him.

The Burlington Free Press and the *Rutland Herald* hit the streets with special afternoon EXTRAS!, providing confirmation of the governor's death to a news-hungry state. The afternoon newspapers held their editions as late as possible to include every available piece of information. Television and radio stations aired special reports.

As we in the press rushed to put together information on the immediate tragedy, we also began to focus on the task of putting into perspective the abruptly ended Snelling years. Others in my office began to pull together information on Dean. He was a little-known Democrat with few political achievements to his credit. A poll released just the previous night had shown that about a third of those polled either did not know Dean or had no opinion of him.

> As we in the press rushed to put together information on the immediate tragedy, we also began to focus on the task of putting into perspective the abruptly ended Snelling years.

Never before had the office of governor switched political parties outside of an election, and that was another element of the story. Vermont's system of independently elected governors and lieutenant governors meant that Democrat Dean was replacing Republican Snelling. Would Dean fire the Snelling Cabinet?

Dean immediately sought to reassure the state. He named Snelling's chief of staff to be his chief of staff; he asked the Snelling staff and Cabinet to remain in office, and he pledged to continue the Snelling plan to erase the state's deficit.

Meanwhile, David Schütz, the long-time curator of the State House, ordered black drapery to be added to the State House's colorful bunting. The Snelling family, however, asked that it be removed.

75

Vermont's birthday was something to celebrate, and they insisted the festivities go forward.

Although Snelling had served in office previously for eight years, between 1977 and 1985, these final eight months of his reincarnation as governor would define his legacy. A fear that Vermont's fiscal crisis would irreparably harm the state prompted Snelling's decision in 1990 to run again for governor. But these eight months in office proved to be far tougher than even Snelling thought they would be when he started his campaign.

A chief executive, Snelling once told me, has to be able to withstand "the attacks, the personal vendettas, the cruel cartoons [to do the job right]. . . . You have to have staying power and confidence." And during his first eight years as governor, Snelling withstood innumerable attacks and countless critical cartoons and editorials, but nothing seemed to hit as hard as all the criticism Snelling endured in his final eight months after regaining the office in 1991.

He had returned to elective politics, bringing his acuity and supreme self confidence, to fix a fiscal problem that had developed while he was not in office. And yet in a state with a long history of fiscal conservatism and balanced budgets, he bore the brunt of the criticism for the tax increases and spending cuts he promoted to maintain that tradition. "It is very unpleasant for a governor, extremely unpleasant," he had told me that March. "Every morning I read the governor wants to cut this or that. I don't want to cut this or cut that, but my task is to lead this very painful process of getting things under control.

"I read 'the governor wants to increase the sales tax' and 'wants to increase the income tax.' I don't want to do that at all. But if I can be part of the cure, and if people somehow or other need to blame somebody, I would rather have that happen than not have the cure happen."

His efforts led to a historic cooperation that surprised us all and forged one of the most unusual partnerships ever seen in the state. On the opening day of the 1991 legislative session, House Speaker Ralph Wright, celebrating his re-election as speaker, sat in his office, laughing with his lieutenants. Wright, a die-hard Democrat, glanced out his door, and there, sitting in the tiny alcove reading a magazine, was Snelling. The speaker, flustered by the rare, unscheduled appearance of a governor, asked his secretary what was going on. The governor would like to see you, but didn't want to interrupt you, she said.

Wright shooed out the House members and invited in the governor. Snelling told the speaker that while everyone expected the two colossal egos to come to blows during the session, they must work together. And he detailed a plan to raise taxes to balance the budget. The plan provided more in taxes than Snelling wished, and put a heavier tax burden on the wealthy than Snelling wished, but these concessions he was willing to make to build support with Wright and the Democrats.

And the two men, based on that meeting, worked together. While efforts in several neighboring states, also facing budget crises, fell apart because lawmakers could not agree on a solution, Vermont enacted a bipartisan package of cuts and tax increases, including $90 million in new revenue, the largest tax hike in the history of the state. The collaboration was possible only because the Republican governor took that first step and offered his hand to the Democratic speaker of the House. Ultimately, that collaboration turned out to demand more of Wright than he could anticipate. When the bill came before the House, the vote on final passage ended up tied—72 in favor and 72 against—forcing Wright to break the tie in favor of the bill.

On that August day in 1991, as I searched for the right words to sum up Snelling, a man with endless energy, unlimited enthusiasm and curiosity and singular determination, I focused on how he tackled every task with missionary zeal. Nothing was too small to excite him; no task too large to dissuade him. In 1980 he thought nothing of starting a national campaign to draft Gerald Ford to run again for president. In 1984 he launched a national campaign to balance the federal budget, enlisting Ford and Jimmy Carter as co-chairmen.

Snelling's interests were varied and sometimes surprising. In 1989, when I visited his Shelburne home to tape an interview for public television, he took me on a tour of his just-completed lawn renovation. He had designed and installed himself the electrical lighting system that ran from the house down to Lake Champlain, and he enthusiastically detailed the books he had consulted and every aspect of his planning. In the newly renovated house he took great pride in showing me how he had determined the level of his new dining room floor using a transit to ensure a clear view of Lake Champlain.

> **[Dean] is the governor who likened the Legislature to a zoo, grumbled that Supreme Court justices think they are God, called the left wing of his party arrogant and the right wing of the Republican Party a bunch of crackpots.**

A few months before he died, when the Legislature was in the midst of its agonizing debate over the state's fiscal crisis, Snelling called me. Although he was seemingly preoccupied prodding and pushing lawmakers to adopt his plan, he wanted me to know that he had just learned his grandmother had worked for the American Press Association, in Washington, for four years. What was that? he inquired. He later discovered that his grandmother, Alice Lee Moque, an author, was a leader of the suffrage movement. With the same enthusiasm he plowed into bringing Canadian power to Vermont, Snelling drank up everything he could find on suffrage and his grandmother.

I told these stories in my tribute to Snelling and concluded that Snelling's place in history was assured, something he always doubted. "If you want to get into the history books, you take a molehill," he once said. "You call it a mountain and move it. Making government productive, making it work, that's not the stuff of which heroes are made."

It is hard to remember today how little we all thought of Dean when he assumed the governor's office in 1991. We now have the perspective of his almost twelve years in office and his presidential run, but in August 1991, most insiders saw him as a lightweight. And a liberal one, at that. Within a week of Snelling's death, talk was already circulating that Dean would only serve out the remaining months of Snelling's term; then Snelling's widow, Barbara, would run for governor in 1992. And initially Dean did little to show he was eager to be governor. In the first few weeks he tried hard to spend as much time as possible with his children, Anne, who was then seven, and Paul, then five, and seemed to be fighting hard to retain as much normalcy as possible in his family's life. He continued to drive his son and daughter to school some days, with a state police cruiser trailing behind. Dean, who was a youthful looking 42 at the time, had consciously decided not to run for governor in 1990, opting to remain in the number two spot, which he described at the time "as the perfect life. It gave me time for patients, politics and family." All this fed rumors that he would not seek the governor's office when the next election rolled around.

At the time of Snelling's death, I likened the day to April 12, 1945, when President Franklin D. Roosevelt's sudden death elevated Harry Truman to the Oval Office. Snelling had been a commanding figure on the state's political landscape. Like Truman, Dean was an unknown. At the time I grabbed the comparison primarily to evoke an image of dramatic change. Over the years, though, the Truman analogy stuck, and when Dean stepped down as governor, I wrote that the comparison held: Howard Dean was Vermont's Harry Truman.

Just like Truman, Dean showed himself to be a no-nonsense, plain-speaking guy who loves to give 'em hell. This is the governor who likened the Legislature to a zoo, grumbled that Supreme Court justices think they are God, called the left wing of his party arrogant and the right wing of the Republican Party a bunch of crackpots.

Dean, like Truman, confronted problems and situations without precedent: In Truman's case it was the dropping of the atomic bomb; in Dean's case it was the cultural landmine of expanding gay rights. The parallels run deeper: Both men won difficult re-elections in which the electorate split over issues of civil rights. In Truman's case, southern Democrats opposed to a strong civil rights program formed the Dixiecrat Party; in Dean's case, opponents of civil unions worked hard for the GOP challenger. Coincidentally, Progressive Party candidates challenged them both.

Few Vermont governors have faced as many crises on their watch: Dean assumed office during the worst recession since the Great Depression (although he also later presided over the longest economic expansion in modern history). Devastating floods, a disastrous ice storm, droughts, near bankruptcies of the electric utilities and much more happened during Dean's tenure. The greatest challenges, though, arose neither from tough economic times nor from natural disasters. They came from coping with court orders. No Vermont governor has ever faced two Supreme Court rulings of such historic import. For a century governors had talked about reforming the state system of financing schools, but Howard Dean was ordered to do so. No other governor in the nation had ever had to implement a law extending the rights and benefits of marriage to gays and lesbians. Again, Howard Dean was ordered to do so, and his legacy as governor will forever be linked with passage and implementation of the civil unions law.

What Vermonters liked best about their doctor governor was that he appeared to be an average guy. Like Truman, who went for a walk every morning at 5:30 and passed most evenings quietly with his family in the White House residence, Dean seemed most comfortable doing everyday things. He was a passionate fan of his children's sports, and whenever he could he arranged his gubernatorial duties to be available to cheer them on in soccer and ice hockey. He also enjoyed hiking the Long Trail and canoeing the Connecticut River. He seemed to genuinely appreciate Vermont's natural beauty and recreational opportunities, in ways that governors before and after him have not, and this resonated within the state, where much of the population shared his interests. Often during long sessions of the Legislature he would pop into the State House to check on things wearing a UVM hockey jacket and snow boots of some kind, on his way to or from skiing with his children.

Also like Truman, Dean reveled in controversy. While Truman hammered the "Do-Nothing Congress," Dean clashed repeatedly with Vermont lawmakers, claiming they spent too much and couldn't say "No." Over his years as governor, Dean angered just about everyone at one point or another: The left, the right, the business community, environmentalists, property rights advocates, doctors, health insurers, farmers and developers all were unhappy with Dean decisions.

He is, by his own admission, "an odd kind of Democrat." When he assumed office he fixated on balancing the budget, but many regarded this as a political necessity already set in stone by his predecessor. Analysts predicted that the true tax-and-spend liberal would emerge once he won election in his own right. It never did. As the years passed, the Dean of 1991 remained: a fiscal conservative, a social moderate and a friend to business interests.

Many of his positions as governor would have surprised some of the supporters of his presidential bid, who considered his anti-war position a fair representation of his philosophy. Take law and order. Phil Hoff once said to me that he wondered if Dean even understood the principle of due process. Dean believed, for example, that the penal system coddles criminals. "People don't get enough time and they get off on technicalities," he said in 1995. "That's wrong. They ought to be in the can. They ought to stay there. Forever." And on this issue, as with many others, Dean's mind was made up. No lessons on the importance of civil rights or the role of the courts or public defenders ever changed it. Sometimes he would hurl one of his zingers, without any regard for to the facts of the matter, such as the time he lambasted the state

Supreme Court for releasing "five murderers in the space of twelve months. They've turned loose five guys." I investigated and found that wasn't true. The court had ordered the release of only one person and had called for new trials in the other four cases.

What I soon learned about Dean, though, was that his positions were often aligned with those of the voters. He had an uncanny ability to see where the public was on any issue and to be there even before Vermonters had articulated their feelings. At the time, many Vermonters did, indeed, feel the courts were soft on criminals; most Vermonters felt government overspent and many of them did suspect the Legislature was a zoo. My complaint with Dean was his eagerness to show disdain for the work of those in government, which, in turn, fostered the feeling generally. After decades of covering state government, I thought it was misleading.

Dean's signature issue was healthcare, and it remained his primary focus throughout his entire tenure as governor. Within a month of taking office he singled out healthcare as a priority, and in a national news interview he urged doctors to become more involved in the political process. "Healthcare is going to be the number one problem over the next five years, and doctors are doing their profession and the public a disservice by not getting into politics," he said. His background as a doctor, one of the few in the top echelons of government nationally, gave him credibility on the issue, both in Vermont and across the country.

A report on healthcare costs prepared by a special commission appointed by Snelling months before his death landed on Dean's desk shortly after he became governor. The 1992 Legislature endorsed the commission's call for creation of an independent healthcare authority to design a new delivery system that would contain costs yet ensure access to healthcare for all. Dean appointed the three members of the authority in July 1992 and, as required, the panel delivered two options to the Legislature late in 1993, one that relied on multiple payers and one that called for a single-payer system. As the 1994 legislative session opened, almost everyone thought major reform of the state healthcare system was just months away from being enacted. House Speaker Ralph Wright appointed a special House committee to consider the measure in hopes of streamlining the process and promoting passage. The plan, though, was incredibly complex, and we in the press had tremendous difficulties understanding the proposal ourselves, much less communicating to the public what was going on. At one point Dean said the new system would cost $37 million, but others estimated the true cost would be more than $100 million, and even then there was talk that healthcare costs would remain high for most families.

> What I soon learned about Dean, though, was that his positions were often aligned with those of the voters. He had an uncanny ability to see where the public was on any issue and to be there even before Vermonters had articulated their feelings.

By mid-March it was clear that the comprehensive bill would not pass the House. In his autobiography, *All Politics is Personal*, Speaker Wright recalls that he turned to Dean when it became evident the bill was mired in the House, hoping to develop a strategy for continuing the fight in the Senate.

"What are we going to do?" Wright asked.

"Nothing," said Dean, in a telling example of his style. "It's dead."

Wright was incredulous. "That's it? IT's dead? Two years of grinding and fighting, and it's dead? Everything went out of my mind, as the only visual I had was the governor in a hospital room, pulling another sheet over a patient's face, and turning to look at the charts on the patient in the next bed."

The collapse of the major healthcare initiative did not deter Dean from continuing to work on the issue. Year after year he promoted and passed some incremental change. By the end of his time as governor all those little changes added up to big successes: Every child in the state was eligible for health insurance, putting Vermont at the top of the list of states providing healthcare for kids.

Running for re-election in 1996 Dean faced his strongest political challenge yet. Barbara Snelling, elected lieutenant governor in 1992 and re-elected in 1994, announced in November 1995 that she would run for governor. The widow of Richard Snelling, she was not one of those wives who had entered politics on her husband's coattails. She would bring to the campaign both her experience in government and an array of skills gleaned from a distinguished career as a vice president at the University of Vermont and as founder and principal in an international consulting business specializing in helping nonprofit organizations with fundraising and public relations.

However, on April 13, 1996, Mrs. Snelling, who was then 68, was attending a meeting of state Republicans in Hartland when she developed an excruciating headache in the back of her neck. She left the meeting room and collapsed. An ambulance rushed her to Dartmouth Hitchcock Medical Center, where doctors said she had suffered a cerebral hemorrhage. Her chances of survival were very slim; only five percent of the people who suffer such strokes survive. But as her son, Mark, told the doctors, "You don't know my mother." A neurosurgeon worked quickly to reduce the pressure in her brain from internal bleeding. Mrs. Snelling remained in a coma for some thirty hours. At one point a broadcast station reported that she had died.

I talked several times that day to Mark Snelling and to Howard Dean, among many others, gathering facts and reactions for the stories we were writing. I remember Mark Snelling's candidness in saying the outlook was not good. I remember, too, how distraught Dean sounded just after hearing the news. Even though Mrs. Snelling was his announced opponent, Dean instantly dispatched his state police trooper to help get the Snelling children as quickly as possible to the hospital in Lebanon, New Hampshire. I also remember another quintessential Vermont moment. Two days later Mrs. Snelling had some follow-up surgery. She was rolled out of the operating room into recovery at the same time as Joan Smith, the wife of Peter Welch, who had been Dick

Snelling's opponent in 1990. The families spent time comforting each other before and during the surgeries, and did so again after. "There is a certain intimacy in a small state," Welch said to me later that week. "You respect the people you disagree with. You expect to see them down the road. And you do."

With Mrs. Snelling's remarkable recovery—she went home on May 8—the big political question of 1996 was whether she would continue her race for governor. Underlying that question, of course, was the issue of her health. After Mrs. Snelling returned home, the Snelling family basically pulled down a veil of privacy. No one outside of the family and a few friends saw her or knew how she was. In early June, though, Mark Snelling invited me to conduct the first interview with her. I did so with some trepidation, because I felt I was being asked to evaluate Mrs. Snelling's ability to serve as lieutenant governor and to continue her campaign for governor. When I arrived, two of her children, Mark and Diane, were waiting for me, and they seemed equally nervous. When their mother arrived we sat and talked about a whole range of issues, while I tried to test her memory and knowledge without being too obvious about it.

In a note I sent to newspaper editors accompanying my article, I wrote of my personal impressions, mentioning that she was "obviously tired, easily distracted, but surprisingly strong" and that "the biggest factor in the decision about her political future is the uncertainty of when she will be fully recovered. Not knowing for sure when her stamina will return makes it difficult for her to judge in June how she could handle the rigors of a gubernatorial campaign." Ultimately, Mrs. Snelling dropped out of the race for governor, but she ran and won a seat in the state Senate from Chittenden County.

In 1998 Mrs. Snelling sought to regain her old office of lieutenant governor. She ran against Doug Racine, whom she had defeated in 1994 but who then won the office in 1996 after Mrs. Snelling's stroke. That election night proved to be a long one. After UPI left the state in 1985, the AP was solely responsible for tabulating election results, and to me fell the job of declaring the winners and losers. The pressure was always incredibly intense, especially as the television stations neared their 11 p.m. newscasts and as the daily newspapers approached their dead-lines, which ranged from midnight to 3 a.m. Between 1980 and 2004, however, I never called an election wrong. Some years were easy, and other years involved agonizingly close contests. The Snelling-Racine race of 1998 was one of the hardest to call, with the two candidates holding pretty even throughout the night. Finally, at 2 a.m., with 800 votes out of some 200,000 votes counted separating the two and with approximately two dozen communities yet to report in, I declared Racine the winner. Whenever I made calls in close contests, I then spent the rest of the night—and actually the rest of the next week until the official vote count was released by the secretary of state—

In June 1997 lawmakers passed what became Act 60, a system of financing schools through a statewide, rather than a local, property tax. At the time, I wrote of the accomplishment that it was an imperfect solution, but an important change

worrying if I was wrong. In the Snelling-Racine matchup the final official results had Racine winning by little more than a thousand votes.

One of the constants throughout Vermont history has been contro-versy over how best to finance schools. Gov. Madeleine Kunin put it bluntly in 1987: "Today in Vermont, the quality of education a child receives depends on where he or she resides." That echoed what gover-nors had been saying for a century. In 1868 Gov. John Page bemoaned that "the burdens of taxation do not bear equally on all classes of prop-erty;" a century later Gov. Deane Davis said that Vermonters most of all wanted their children to have the opportunity for a good education "regardless of whether he lives in a rich or poor family and regardless of whether he lives in a rich or poor town." Nevertheless, the problem per-sisted down the decades, leading me to conclude over time that property tax reform probably fell into that category of problems so politically and emotionally charged that they would remain unresolved until the courts forced changed. And that's exactly what happened.

On February 5, 1997, the Vermont Supreme Court finally ruled unconstitutional the system of requiring towns to finance the education of their children. "The distribution of a resource as precious as educational opportunity may not have as its determining force the mere fortuity of a child's residence. It requires no particular constitutional expertise to recognize the capriciousness of such a system," the justices ruled. What struck me about the court decision was its clarity and passion. The justices cut through the complexities and confusion that swirl around education financing to remind us of a basic fact: Education is about opportunity, and kids and their future. "To keep a democracy competitive and thriving, students must be afforded equal access to all that our educational system has to offer," the court said. The system is broken, the court said. Stop yapping and do something.

In June 1997 lawmakers passed what became Act 60, a system of financing schools through a statewide, rather than a local, property tax. At the time, I wrote of the accomplishment that it was an imperfect solution, but an important change:

> Will it work? No one can say for sure. It is immensely complex, more so than necessary, perhaps. It will not provide the levels of property tax relief some had hoped. But more so than any thought possible, it is going to make the "mere fortuity of a child's residence" less of a factor in the quality of education.
>
> Will it stand up in court? Most likely. Challenges will come from many corners, but it is extremely likely the Supreme Court will reject them.
>
> Will it be changed? You bet. The imperfections are many and well known, but lawmakers consider this a work-in-progress and revisions will be an annual affair.
>
> But no matter how much it is changed in the future, the system of financing schools will never again be what it is now.

As lawmakers cobbled together Act 60, no one anticipated the outrage that would come from the communities Deane Davis had called "the rich towns." Those communities that host ski areas or major businesses, like IBM, had been able to finance high-quality schools with low local property taxes. Act 60 ended that sweet deal, and residents in those towns rose up in protest, fearing that their schools would be gutted under a new system that siphoned off some of their tax revenue for schools in towns without similarly expensive homes and prosperous businesses. "This is civil war," said Bob Stannard, a former House member who was lobbying for the gold towns. In the national press, *The New York Times* depicted Vermont as a state divided, where "The social fabric of Vermont is fraying. The divisions that exist in all societies—between rich and poor, employer and employee, young and old, insiders and outsiders—are widening into chasms. And Vermont's mythic sense of itself as a special community seems increasingly at stake." The article quoted the hyperbole of a Stowe realtor, who said, "This is the great rape. I think there will be blood in the streets." A Manchester auto mechanic cautioned, "They're going to start a revolution. I think we should have another Boston Tea Party." After one meeting in Manchester, in which one of the Act 60 architects, Sen. Peter Shumlin, told the audience, "I don't blame you for not liking Act 60. You had a great deal, and it's coming to an end," an opponent of the change, Mary Barrosse, said of the tension in the room, "It makes me feel like someone is going to get shot." Novelist John Irving, whose son then attended kindergarten in Dorset, raised the profile of the state even higher by denouncing the law as "Marxism. It levels everything by decimating what works."

In 1998 lawmakers made some changes to Act 60 to ease the burden on the property wealthy towns, but opponents kept up their fight. The state Republican Party embraced the anti-Act 60 movement as its own: The GOP released a series of television ads designed to rekindle the anti-Act 60 fire. One showed wheelbarrows of money going from a town to Montpelier and returning empty. Republican gubernatorial candidate Ruth Dwyer, a state representative from Thetford, campaigned hard against Act 60, using the law's shortcomings as a symbol of how government had lost its way and the statewide property tax as a symbol of an over-reaching state government. Nevertheless, in November the Democrats held onto the Legislature, and Dean defeated Dwyer 56 percent to 42 percent.

In 1999 the Supreme Court would again issue a historic decision, one that would again tear at the social fabric of the state, again put Howard Dean on the defensive and again give Ruth Dwyer volatile ammunition with which to challenge Dean. That decision declared unconstitutional the state's laws denying gays and lesbians the rights and benefits of marriage. Vermont would never be the same.

Between the decisions on Act 60 and civil unions came a significant change in the makeup of the Supreme Court. Richard Snelling's choice for chief justice, Frederic Allen, retired, and to take his place Dean appointed Attorney General Jeffrey Amestoy, a Republican. At the news conference at which Dean announced his appointment, reporters asked Amestoy when he learned he was the governor's choice. He answered, "Just after Chris Graff did, I think." That was a delicious moment for me. Dean's search for a chief justice had been particularly difficult when he rejected the first list of nominees selected by the state Judicial Nominating Board. The governor believed the panel was too strict in its review of applicants and had unfairly shut out those who lacked experience on the bench, including Dean's favorite, William Sorrell, a former Chittenden County state's attorney who at the time was Dean's secretary of administration. Thirteen people had applied in that first round and only two—Justices John Dooley and James Morse—passed muster with the board. After Dean's scathing attacks on the Supreme Court during his years in office, there was little chance he was going to appoint one of those two. The Judicial Nominating Board started again.

Using sources I had developed over two decades of covering the courts, I was able to report on the search every step of the way, even though proceedings of the Judicial Nominating Board are secret. During the first search, I broke the news that Sorrell had been scratched by the board. Later I reported that Amestoy had applied in the second round, and eventually I was first with news of his appointment—even before he had heard officially from the governor.

The different styles of governors were most evident at news conferences. Some, like Tom Salmon, tended to focus more on the big picture of governing, deferring to Cabinet secretaries to answer questions if reporters pressed for details; others, like Dick Snelling, turned the news conferences into personal tours de force, using each question as a springboard for a lesson on the complexities of the world and the correctness of his vision. Howard Dean was a showman: His news conferences were theatrical performances during which the audience sat on the edge of its seat wondering what he might say. He rarely disappointed. Sometimes he would announce new policies at news conferences, changes that he had yet to discuss with his staff or department heads. Signs of these bombshells came when he paused in his answer, looked over to his chief of staff or press secretary and then announced, "My staff will kill me for saying this, but. . . ." Other times Dean would simply vent. Some of his most memorable zingers—such as when he likened the Legislature to a zoo—were born in the heat of remarks during news conferences.

Dean's memory is dazzling. Time and again he demonstrated his ability to call up on demand even the most arcane facts and minutia of state government. He loved to strut his stuff at news conferences and in interviews. I host "Call The Governor" on Vermont Public Television, in which viewers phone in and have the opportunity to ask the governor any question they wish. Dean always seemed to relish the off-beat questions, the ones that allowed him to show his knowledge.

Sometimes, though, even he was stumped. I remember a program we did in 1998, when a caller from Lyndonville asked him what he was going to do about the influx of carpenter ants. He told her he didn't know what to do about his own carpenter ant problem, much less hers. Hosting that program taught me a great deal about what matters to people. I would come to the show expecting questions on the major policy debates before the Legislature, only to find that viewers were more concerned with issues affecting their lives more directly, such as their property tax bills, child care needs or rising energy costs. Another time Dean was at a loss was during the National Governors Association meeting in Burlington in 1995. C-SPAN's Brian Lamb was interviewing Dean, and Dean showed his usual finesse in answering complex queries about Medicaid formulas and welfare waivers. He drew a blank, however, when Lamb asked him to name the state motto. "I don't know," Dean confessed. "I think it's Latin." For others who don't know, the motto is "Freedom and Unity."

> Dean's memory is dazzling. Time and again he demonstrated his ability to call up on demand even the most arcane facts and minutia of state government. He loved to strut his stuff at news conferences and in interviews.

Over time I grew accustomed to governors and their aides calling me at home, but they were not the only government employees to do so. Somewhere around 2 a.m. on a Tuesday in January, in 1998, my telephone rang at home. The person at the other end didn't identify himself. He didn't have to. His was perhaps the most recognizable voice in Vermont. He told me a building in the center of downtown Montpelier was burning. Thought I'd like to know. I said "Thanks, Ray," hung up and went down to report on a fire that nearly destroyed a four-story building that had anchored a corner of Montpelier since 1826. The caller was Ray Burke, who spent 32 years telling Vermonters things he thought they ought to know. Ray, who retired in 2002, was the state highway dispatcher, a title that didn't begin to do justice to all he did. Vermonters spend their whole lives wondering if they can get there from here. Ray helped us figure that out, telling us when to drive and when not to, where to expect construction delays and when accidents had closed down highways. He did it all with good cheer. No matter how bad the weather, Ray found a sunny side: "Snow makes Vermont go," he reminded us in the midst of a blizzard. "After it's all over with, you get all the out-of-staters here to go skiing."

On September 5, 2001, Dean announced he would not seek re-election. "The baton has to be passed sometime," he said at a news conference on the State House lawn.

For decades our first call at The Associated Press when road conditions deteriorated was to Ray, and we were not alone. Most radio and television stations checked in with Ray, and for almost twenty years Ray did a live morning highway and road report at 7:40 on Waterbury radio station WDEV. His folksy chats with station manager Eric Michaels were as much about his Berlin farm or his saxophone playing as they were about the roads, and they were often interrupted as Ray carried on separate conversations with the drivers of state highway trucks around the state. He knew all the roads in the state in detail and could figure out how elevation changes would affect what kind of precipitation would fall where, an especially impressive feat because Ray couldn't really look at a forecast. He is blind; a hereditary disease cost him his sight in the 1960s when he was working in the state highway department laboratory. Ray's commitment to the job was legendary: He worked 54 hours straight during the 1973 flood. He often slept in the office, and played his guitar over the highway department radio channel to keep snowplow drivers awake on the overnight shift.

Ray followed into retirement another legend: Ray Kelley, who for two decades kept Vermonters from freezing. When the mercury plunged, Kelley crisscrossed the state, doing whatever it took to keep Vermonters warm and safe. His title was welfare emergency assistance specialist. He was the guy folks turned to when their oil tanks went dry and they didn't have the money to refill them, or when trouble hit after regular business hours. His toughest task was meeting those needs in the bitter cold nights that are difficult for all Vermonters to endure, but especially so for the most vulnerable. Some winter nights the state hot line would receive more than 150 calls, each with a story of terror, an elderly person or a family with children facing the darkness in the cold. One such call came from neighbors of an elderly woman on the other side of the state, in St. Albans. They thought she was without heat, and the temperature was 38 degrees below zero. Kelley climbed in his car and drove to the woman's home, where he found her wrapped up in blankets and coats.

On September 5, 2001, Dean announced he would not seek re-election. "The baton has to be passed sometime," he said at a news conference on the State House lawn. "I have accomplished many things that I wanted to accomplish in this job. What we have done is extraordinary." A reflection of the man can be seen in what topped his list. It wasn't the dramatic expansion of healthcare for children, or the traumatic birth of civil unions, or his strict fiscal management or even the revolutionary change in financing education. Dean cited land conservation as his greatest good. "A hundred years from now we will have hunting, hiking, fishing and snowmobile riding because of what we did," he said. He had plenty to brag about: No governor has come close to Dean in engineering the purchase of development rights on farms, giving farmers cash to stay in business, and brokering a massive deal to conserve 133,000 acres of recreation and timberland in the Northeast Kingdom.

He admitted at the news conference that he had leaned toward a 2002 run when it seemed as if the state's fiscal problems were going to be more serious than they were turning out to be. He said he was not sure what he would do next; my guess at the time was that he would run for Jim Jeffords' U.S. Senate seat in 2006. Soon, though, Dean began to lay the groundwork for his presidential bid.

In 2002, Dean's lame-duck status, combined with extensive travels in his presidential bid, caught up with him at the State House. He had told reporters that his staff was so full of seasoned veterans that no one would even notice his absences. But people did notice his rare appearances, because he too often dropped in and let loose with some explosive comment before jetting off, leaving angry lawmakers in his wake. Once in May he stopped in at the State House long enough to complain that "the Senate budget is in la-la land" and that senators "did not have the spine" to make the needed tough budget choices. His criticism was directed at the Democrats who controlled the Senate, and they were not happy. Sen. Peter Shumlin, the president pro tem, fired back with comments dripping in sarcasm: "It's thoughtful of the governor to stop by for a few hours and share his thoughts on the budget." Shumlin added, "The governor's running for president. I'm trying to run the Senate. Vermonters will have to decide who's trespassing closer to the border of la-la land." At that point, according to the lieutenant governor's office, Dean had been out of state 63 of 128 days, a sure sign of his focus and the reason the lawmakers were frustrated.

In January 2003, at Dean's final news conference as governor, I gave him, on behalf of the Montpelier press corps, a puzzle of the United States to help him with his geography as he crossed the country in his presidential bid, as well as a map of Iowa to guide him through the state's 99 counties. At the end of the news conference he talked about his presidential race. He seemed surprised that someone had recently recognized him on his travels. "I have assumed I'm going to run around the subway with a suitcase and nobody's going to worry about who I am or pay attention to me," he said. "Of course, that's not going to happen."

I spoke up: "If they don't start recognizing you, Governor, come home."

"I'll tell you something, Chris. No matter what happens, this will always be home."

Crowds protest the bill that would legalize same-sex civil unions.

"We were the first state to outlaw slavery in 1777. We will remain in the forefront of the struggle for equal justice under the law."

— *Gov. Howard Dean*

Chapter 6

The Tempest over Civil Unions

I typed "BULLETIN" and then erased it. I paused and typed "FLASH," signaling to the news world that the upcoming news was of utmost importance. In 21 years with the AP, I had never used the "FLASH" priority. It's reserved for such momentous events as man landing on the moon and the assassination of JFK. I typed on:

> MONTPELIER, Vt. (AP) – Vermont Supreme Court extends rights and benefits of marriage to same sex couples.

With a quickly typed computer command and a push of a button, the "FLASH" moved on the AP wire at 11:04, Monday morning, December 20, 1999. Flush with the adrenaline rush that accompanies a major breaking story, I wrote feverishly, moving a longer "BULLETIN" on the wire two minutes after the brief "FLASH." Within five minutes, I had a 181-word story on the wire that summed up the decision this way:

MONTPELIER, Vt. (AP) – Gay and lesbian couples must be granted the same benefits and protections given married couples of the opposite sex, the Vermont Supreme Court ruled today. But the court stayed its ruling to allow the Legislature to consider whether those benefits will come through marriage or a system of domestic partnerships.

I added 344 words to the story at 11:18, another 218 words at 11:23 and then combined that so-called "URGENT" series into one updated 849-word story at 11:32, just half an hour after the court released its decision.

Amazingly, I had not even read the court decision. But I had gotten what I needed to file the initial report simply by glancing at the cover sheet that contained the court's order and at the first page, which said the court would stay its order to allow lawmakers to respond to the ruling.

This case was more difficult to decipher than most Supreme Court decisions because the justices issued three opinions: a 45-page majority opinion written by Chief Justice Jeffrey Amestoy; an 18-page concurring opinion by Justice John Dooley and a 30-page opinion by Justice Denise Johnson, concurring in part and dissenting in part. Working for a wire service, I did not have the luxury of time to sort through all of the decisions because I had to file something immediately. Speed was critical. But so was accuracy. My interpretation of this case would be the first word the world would hear on the outcome.

And there is no doubt the world was waiting. Justice Dooley called this case "the most closely watched opinion in this court's history." Justice Johnson wrote that "this case is undoubtedly one of the most controversial ever to come before this court." As a sign of the case's significance, my story would top the AP's national news digest for Tuesday's newspapers. Two days later *The New York Times* would headline its editorial on the decision "Vermont's Momentous Ruling." According to the editorial, the Vermont Supreme Court had "awarded the gay rights movement its biggest victory so far in the struggle to achieve legal recognition and acceptance for same-sex marriages."

The case began in the summer of 1997 when three couples—two lesbian and one gay—filed suit in Chittenden County Superior Court after being denied marriage licenses by their respective local town clerks. The clerks acted on the advice of the state attorney general, who relied, in turn, on a 1975 opinion by a predecessor calling same-sex marriages unconstitutional. The couples argued that their inability to marry denied them more than 300 benefits at the state level and more than 1,000 at the federal level. The benefits varied from access to a spouse's health insurance and hospital visitation to the right to certain survivor and spousal benefits.

> Justice Dooley called this case "the most closely watched opinion in this court's history." Justice Johnson wrote that "this case is undoubtedly one of the most controversial ever to come before this court."

The trial court dismissed their suit, ruling that the state's marriage statutes were constitutional. Although the judge, Linda Levitt, rejected many of the state's arguments, she determined the marriage laws were in keeping with Vermont's interest in promoting "the link between procreation and child rearing." The couples appealed to the state Supreme Court, and on November 18, 1998, a Wednesday morning, the five justices listened to arguments. The small courtroom was packed, and the audio of the proceedings was broadcast to the overflow gathered in the lobby just outside the courtroom. Never had so many people showed up at the court for an oral argument.

The formal name of the case—docket No. 98-032—was *Stan Baker, et al. v. State of Vermont, et al.* Stan Baker was one of the six plaintiffs in the case. At its center were three same-sex couples who had lived together in periods ranging from four to twenty-four years; two of the couples had raised children together. In a further example of the state's smallness, I had first met Stan Baker in 1975, when he and his wife, Priscilla, ran a pre-school at their home in Vergennes and my wife gave swimming lessons to the children. In 1993, however, the couple separated, and Stan began life as a gay man.

Generally, the court takes between six and twelve months to decide a case. Beginning in the summer of 1999, therefore, I geared up the bureau every Friday to be ready for the decision. The Supreme Court routinely releases its decisions at 11 a.m. on Fridays, and so I made sure that either Ross Sneyd, the reporter who covered the case, or I was in the bureau at that time in case the Baker decision came down. In this instance, however, the court broke with tradition, probably because the justices wanted to get the decision out before the end of the year but preferred not to release it on Friday, Christmas Eve. To everyone's surprise, the decision came on a Monday, showing that even diligent planning cannot fully prepare reporters for the unpredictability of news. Fortunately, I was in the bureau when word came from the court.

I filed two more updates to the story, with new reaction, by 12:19 p.m. Then I finally sat down to read through the complete decision and the two companion opinions. Paging through the 93 pages left me with the clear impression that the full court felt no legal or constitutional reason existed to restrict marriage in Vermont to a union between a man and a woman. All that prevented the court from ordering gay marriage, in my reading, was a belief by four of the five justices that Vermonters would not readily accept it. The justices seemed to recognize that just their ruling giving gay and lesbian couples the same rights, benefits and protections as heterosexual couples was sufficiently groundbreaking for Vermonters to grapple with in one day. "Our decision declares decidedly new doctrine," wrote Amestoy. "A sudden change in the marriage laws or the statutory benefits traditionally incidental to marriage may have disruptive and unforeseen consequences."

Four of the justices — all but Johnson — were wary of having the judiciary act as a legislature. To me it was especially telling that Amestoy quoted in his opinion from an article in the *Harvard Law Review*: "When a democracy is in moral flux, courts may not have the best or final answers. Judicial answers may be wrong. They may be counterproductive even if they are right." The Vermont justices apparently felt they would be right to order same-sex marriage, but they feared a public backlash that might ultimately trample the rights of gays and lesbians. Therefore, they would paint the picture in broad strokes and let the Legislature fill in the details. That's where Johnson objected. If there is a wrong, we need to right it, she said: "The majority, in effect, issues an advisory opinion that leaves plaintiffs without redress and sends the matter to an uncertain fate in the Legislature."

During this full reading of the decisions, I came across the sentence that would become the most widely quoted passage: The extension of the state Constitution's common benefit clause "to acknowledge plaintiffs as Vermonters who seek nothing more, nor less, than legal protection and security for their avowed commitment to an intimate and lasting human relationship is simply, when all is said and done, a recognition of our common humanity."

Ross Sneyd, the AP's political and State House reporter who had been covering the case since its original filing, went to a news conference hastily called by the plaintiffs and their lawyers in South Burlington. Everyone had been caught off guard by the timing of the decision. Peter Harrigan, one of the plaintiffs, was on his way to Kmart to shop for Christmas when he heard the initial report on the radio.

What was surprising — in light of the divisive debate that would fracture the state in the coming year — was how upbeat both sides seemed after the release of the decision. Mary Bonauto, a Boston lawyer who worked on the case for the plaintiffs, called the ruling "a legal and cultural milestone." Stan Baker said, "It's just incredible to have this day come." Opponents, for their part, seemed pleased the court had not endorsed gay marriage. Bishop Kenneth Angell called the ruling "a decisive victory for traditional marriage."

Any hope that an effort to pass legislation without a tough fight, however, evaporated by the start of the 2000 Legislature just two weeks later. Bishop Angell's rhetoric had turned strident. He now condemned domestic partnerships as "step one toward full acceptance of same-sex marriage." He challenged the validity of the Supreme Court ruling, itself, saying in his call to arms to Catholics, "There are many sound legal minds who question the Supreme Court's authority to even issue such mandates to the legislature." At the same time the flush of victory was fading for gays and lesbians, who now believed a system of domestic partnerships would be insufficient to meet the spirit of the Supreme Court ruling. A domestic partner, said one gay, sounds like someone who cleans the house.

> The stepped-up security at the State House on opening day of the 2000 legislative session was more disturbing than reassuring. The dozens of state police troopers...sheriff's deputies and Capitol Police officers stationed throughout the house of the people seemed distinctly wrong.

The stepped-up security at the State House on opening day of the 2000 legislative session was more disturbing than reassuring. The dozens of state police troopers, Washington County sheriff's deputies and Capitol Police officers stationed throughout the house of the people seemed distinctly wrong. The beauty of the Vermont State House lay in it being absolutely and completely open; until the start of the 2000 legislature, Vermonters had always been able to wander in and out of every room, chat with lawmakers and watch democracy in action or inaction. Lawmakers had done their work free of fear. Now all that changed. Fear wormed its way through the halls, and some lawmakers even received death threats. The House Judiciary Committee conducted most of its meetings with a sheriff's deputy standing along the wall.

As the Legislature convened, Gov. Howard Dean delivered his state of the state address with a speech that blended the historic moment of the new millennium with the issues of the day. Standing before the combined representatives and senators, Dean called on lawmakers to respond to the ruling of the high court. "This is the year that we will make every effort to comply with the new Supreme Court ruling, which confirms that all Vermonters—including gay and lesbian Vermonters—are to have equal benefits under the law. We were the first state to outlaw slavery in 1777. We will remain in the forefront of the struggle for equal justice under the law."

Dean had made his position known within an hour of the Supreme Court ruling. "It's in the best interests of all Vermonters, gay and straight, to go forward with the domestic partnership act and not the gay marriage act. And that's what I intend to do," Dean said on that December Monday in yet another hastily called press conference. Asked about his feelings on gay marriage, Dean replied, "It makes me uncomfortable, the same as anyone else." Gay activists would criticize the governor for that statement, but Dean, writing in his 2004 book, *You Have The Power*, defended his comment:

> I was immediately criticized, but I thought it was worthwhile to be honest. After all, like many Americans, I had lived almost all of my life in a culture that was pretty anti-gay. Like a lot of other Americans, I'd snickered at the locker-room jokes, listened to my parents and teachers and ministers, and picked up a lot of things about gay people that weren't nice or true. However, having grown up during the civil rights movement, I also believed that equal rights under the law could not be abridged no matter what I thought about gay marriage.

Crafting the initial legislative response to the Supreme Court fell to the House Judiciary Committee, seven men and four women, a mix of conservatives, moderates and liberals. Some were divorced, some married, some single and one gay man in a committed relationship. Two were former police officers, three were lawyers, several were active in non-profit or social work.

The chair was Tom Little, a Republican who can trace his family back some seven or eight generations in Vermont. At a time when even some Democrats were trying to avoid addressing the topic directly by urging the creation of a commission to study the issue—which would report back after the 2000 elections—Little never flinched. He came into the session prepared to tackle the task at hand and never wavered. On the opening day of the legislative session, he told his committee, "I ask your assistance, advice, good judgment and team work in this important, perhaps monumental, task." And he showed a strength of character. Facing hostile questioning at the House Republican caucus, he could easily have put the blame for the bill on the Court, but he did not hide behind the justices. He told his colleagues that this was the right thing to do—regardless of the Supreme Court decision.

Little's committee, together with the Senate Judiciary Committee, scheduled a public hearing on the issue for January 25. As the day neared, we were hearing of bus caravans planned to bring people from all corners of the state. A heavy snowstorm moved in and the committees decided to go ahead with the hearing, for those who made it, but the expectations were that few would. To everyone's surprise, more than a thousand, perhaps as many as 1,500, showed up—despite the snow. Roughly 500 squeezed into the House chamber for the hearing, while the rest sat on the floors of the ornate reception areas, the cafeteria and hearing rooms, listening to the testimony piped through the building. People wore their opinions on their jackets or shirts, with pink circles declaring "I Support The Freedom to Marry" and white ovals with blue lettering that said "Don't Mock Marriage." The hearing was broadcast statewide, allowing Vermonters of all political and social backgrounds to hear the scripture readings, the passion, the division. They also got to hear from the real people whose lives would be most affected by the legislative action.

I remember clearly walking through the State House that night and seeing every room crammed with people, supporters of gay marriage sitting next to opponents, with everyone listening intently, straining, in fact, to hear the testimony through the sound system. It remains one of the most memorable moments of my more than thirty years in the building. In a news analysis about that night I wrote:

> Donna Lescoe of Starksboro had a simple message for legislators when she testified during the public hearing on gay marriage.
>
> "Be heroes," she said, urging lawmakers to have the courage to extend the marriage laws to include gays and lesbians.
>
> If it were only so simple.
>
> It is hard to be a hero, especially when you are a politician, your political career is on the line, and the divisions are so deep.
>
> The lawmakers looked like anything but heroes following Tuesday night's public hearing. They appeared to be shell-shocked, actually.
>
> Perhaps never before have 1,500 people attended a public hearing at the State House. And the number would have been thousands more if a snowstorm had not kept many away.
>
> Yes, everyone who spoke was civil. But the civility did not mask the passion. Or the division. The tremors in people's voices, a mixture of nerves and emotion, spoke volumes about the depths of feeling.

I concluded the analysis by saying, "The task facing lawmakers is not easy. It is nothing less than living up to the state's motto of 'Freedom and Unity.' How to give gays and lesbians their freedom and yet preserve the unity of the state? It is the stuff heroes are made of."

A second public hearing a week later filled the State House with more than two thousand people, while at least another 1,500 staged a vigil and protest rally outside. A few days after that, Randall Terry swept into town, and the temperature of the debate rose significantly. Terry, from New York state, was a nationally known instigator best known for his militant protests against abortion. However, this issue also apparently pressed his buttons. He rented an office on State Street, two doors down from our office, and announced that he would broadcast his nationally syndicated talk show from Vermont until the civil union debate was settled. He held a news conference on February 3 to detail his protest plans in Vermont, and I decided to attend. I did so only partly to hear Terry; I was more interested in seeing how Ross Sneyd was holding up.

Ross had been the AP's State House reporter for years. Before he came to work for us in Montpelier, he had worked for the AP in Providence, and before that he had been with *The Burlington Free Press*. Ross is an absolute pro, perfectly suited for a wire service. He turns out copy faster than most people can think. He can sit in the House gallery and write a story while a bill is being debated. The story is on the wire as soon as the speaker announces the results of the vote. Ross covered the 2004 presidential campaign, traveling with Howard Dean and later with John Edwards through the New Hampshire primary. The AP later sent Ross to New Orleans to help in the coverage of Hurricane Katrina.

The gay marriage debate added an unusual and personal twist for Ross, because he is gay. Opponents of gay marriage directed some of their ire over general press coverage of the debate at Ross, claiming his stories were biased because he was gay. I listened to every complaint and asked each critic to show me a specific story by Ross that they felt was untrue or unfair. No one ever could. My worry was not over Ross' ability to cover the story fairly and accurately but a personal concern over how he was holding up being on the receiving end of such strong criticism. Randall Terry had already complained about Ross to me and referred to him in statements as "the homosexual reporter."

I walked over to Terry's news conference, therefore, and watched as he denounced homosexuality while Ross stood three feet in front of him. "It is always a tragic, sinful behavior," said Terry. "It is an unnatural, sad, tragic lifestyle." I asked Ross later that day how he was doing. I told him then, as I did several more times that year, that he did not have to cover the issue if he didn't want to. However, he never wavered in his desire to stay with this most historic story, nor did he ever drop his professionalism.

No one is quite sure how or where the phrase "civil unions" originated. In looking through AP copy, I cannot find the term used in February—when the phrase domestic partnerships is used—but it starts appearing in copy in early March. Some say that Rep. Cathy Voyer came up with the phrase as the House Judiciary Committee struggled to find a name for this parallel track to marriage.

The debate around the state was getting less civil as the committee crafted the bill and it started through the legislative process. The situation was inflamed, in part, by all the protests coming from outside the state. Terry urged his radio listeners to call the governor's office and the State House—and the state phone systems were unable to cope with the thousands of incoming calls.

> **"I wish you'd left your New York morals behind when you came to Vermont,"** one Highgate resident told the governor. **"It is a sin. Common sense tells you it is,"** said another Vermonter.

On Town Meeting Day, Gov. Dean ran into repeated and heated complaints about the proposal. "I wish you'd left your New York morals behind when you came to Vermont," one Highgate resident told the governor. "It is a sin. Common sense tells you it is," said another Vermonter at the Fairfield meeting.

The bill came to the House floor in mid-March, prompting two days of passionate and heated debate by lawmakers. Roughly eight hours into the first day of debate, Rep. Bill Lippert rose. A hush fell over the chamber. Lippert, the only openly gay member of the Legislature, as well as a member of the Judiciary Committee, told his colleagues, "I think it's important to put a face on this."

"Gay and lesbian people, gay and lesbian couples, deserve not only rights, they deserve to be celebrated," he said. "Our lives, in the midst of historical prejudice and discrimination, are, in my view, in some way miracles. . . . The goodness of gay and lesbian people, gay and lesbian couples, is a triumph against discrimination and prejudice. We deserve to be welcomed because, in fact, we are your neighbors, your friends, indeed, we are your family."

Almost before Lippert concluded, Rep. Bob Kinsey, R-Craftsbury, was on his feet. "I just heard the greatest speech I've heard in my thirty years," he said. "And that's why I'm glad to be a friend of the member from Hinesburg and that's why I'm glad to be on his side." Kinsey, who was born in Barton, grew up on a farm. He was elected to the House in 1970, and by 2000 had served fifteen terms. Notwithstanding his extensive voting records on thousands of items, he would be one of the lawmakers who would lose his seat in November because of his vote favoring civil unions.

Another Republican voting yes that day was Rep. Marion Milne, then 65, a Republican from the small town of Washington. "Depending on how we vote, this decision may cost some of us our political careers," she said in her floor speech. "If I am measured only by this one vote in my entire political life, I have served my constituents well by voting for this bill. I will not be silenced by hatred and intolerance." She, too, would lose her seat for supporting civil unions.

The anger that would lead to the defeat of Milne, Kinsey and others was festering as the House passed civil unions and sent it to the Senate. The "Take Back Vermont" slogan was still to come, but the movement had a face: Ruth Dwyer, the Thetford state representative who had challenged Howard Dean in 1998, was making another bid for governor, and where Act 60 had fueled the 1998 campaign, civil unions would fuel this one. This change, she declared, "would tear this state apart." In March, as the Senate worked on the bill, Dwyer spoke to a group of Franklin County Republicans and accused Dean of bribing House members to get their votes on civil unions. "The governor is very willing to threaten people, bribe people, anything he can do to get a vote," she said. "If you don't elect people who have the integrity to respect the legislators enough not to threaten and bribe, you're always going to have issues passing the House and Senate that never should have passed." Dwyer later said the use of the word bribery was simply another word for deal-making. Bribery, though, has a very specific connotation, far more serious than deal-making.

In late April the measure came up for vote in the Senate. The lawmakers bared their souls in a deeply emotional and intensely personal, heartwrenching debate. Senators recounted in great eloquence their own personal journeys to reach their decisions, journeys that led nineteen of them to support civil unions and eleven to oppose them. For none was this easy. All were painfully aware the state was divided.

• Sen. Dick McCormack: "What is being asked of us is very little. What we are about to do is terribly important."

• Sen. Hull Maynard: "We have many bewildered people out there. I think my vote for no on this would be to ask for more time to bring this tiny state together."

• Sen. Cheryl Rivers: "The people seldom speak in one voice. They have not been speaking with one voice on this issue."

• Sen. Dick Sears: "I can't tell you all the things I have been called at home. What we have is a state with a lot of fear, a lot of unknown. We fight change."

• Sen. Julius Canns: "This is not a civil rights problem. This is a sex problem."

• Sen. Jim Leddy: "I live in the community I was born in, raised in and grew up in. It is difficult and painful to be accused of betraying my values, betraying my faith, betraying my parents, my family and my heritage."

On April 26, Howard Dean, surrounded only by his staff, signed the civil unions bill into law. He said he did so in private in recognition of the divisions in the state on the merits of the law. Later that afternoon at a news conference, he spoke without notes about what the new law meant to him. "I think the bill that the Legislature crafted does more than simply meet the mandate of the court. I think it is a courageous and powerful statement about who we are in the state of Vermont. I believe what the Legislature has crafted speaks to the notion that the founding fathers of this state put in the Constitution in 1777, that all people are created equal. I also believe that this legislation speaks to the heart of this state, certainly to my heart, because as I've said in the past, we in this state value who we are much more than what we are.

"This bill enriches not just the very small percentage of gay and lesbian Vermonters who take advantage of this partnership and get the rights that the court has determined that they are due. I believe this bill enriches all of us, as we look with new eyes at a group of people who have been outcasts for many, many generations."

> Even as Gov. Dean spoke, the signs were appearing. At first they appeared on a few barns in Orange County. Soon they showed up as lawn signs, and they eventually spread like pollen throughout the state. TAKE BACK VERMONT, they shouted in bold black letters.

Even as Dean spoke the signs were appearing. At first they appeared on a few barns in Orange County. Soon they showed up as lawn signs, and they eventually spread like pollen throughout the state. TAKE BACK VERMONT, they shouted in bold black letters. A farmer in Washington, Richard Lambert, came up with the idea and the design. Soon proponents would counter with signs saying "MOVE VERMONT FORWARD." The debate grew so acrimonious that next came bumper stickers pleading, "Keep Vermont Civil."

Dean's advisers urged him to make a televised speech to calm the state. He finally decided to sit down with me for a live television broadcast on Vermont Public Television devoted entirely to civil unions. He spoke frankly and directly to those upset by civil unions, telling them it was okay to oppose the law — "This is a sea change for many, many people." He believed opponents "have genuine concerns about what this bill will mean to their lives." But Dean added, "I am not going to do anything that I think would harm this state — ever."

The governor argued that those who believed the lawmakers failed to listen to them were wrong. The lawmakers listened, said Dean. They wrestled. They read the Supreme Court decision. They heard the testimony. They received thousands of e-mails, letters and phone calls. In the end, each lawmaker did what he or she thought was the right thing. "This is one time you can be proud of your legislators, not because they are voting a certain way, for or against the bill, but because this debate is about conviction."

In May, Dean startled the party faithful when he opened his speech at the state Democratic Party convention by saying, "I'm going to start out by praising Republicans. There were some extraordinary exhibitions of courage by Republicans in the Legislature this year." However, Dean's praise was not enough to save many of the Republicans who voted for civil unions. Dwyer, the state party chairman and the leaders of the Republican campaigns for the Legislature all lined up against civil unions.

In July Dick Mallary came by my office to drop off a statement. Mallary, the former Republican speaker of the House who had spoken to my eighth grade class at the State House, the former member of the U.S. House who had lost to Pat Leahy in the 1974 Senate race, had returned to elective politics in 1998 by running for the state House. He had been one of the fifteen House Republicans who voted for civil unions. An opponent of civil unions was running against him in the GOP primary. Mallary's statement said he had decided to leave the Republican Party and run as an independent. "For almost fifty years I have actively participated in government and political activity and for all that time I have called myself a Republican," he said. He worried that some leaders of the party were abandoning the GOP's traditional principles "of equal rights, justice and opportunity for all . . . . Furthermore, this year some people are making a concerted effort to purge the party of candidates who voted to honor the order of the court and authorize civil unions in Vermont."

It didn't help. In November Dick Mallary was ousted. And he was far from alone among the civil unions supporters who faced a backlash. Seven senators and 29 Representatives who voted for the law either retired or were defeated. The Republicans took control of the House, but Dean was re-elected and the Democrats held on to the Senate.

The center of the TAKE BACK VERMONT movement was Orange County — the county where Marion Milne and Dick Mallary fell to defeat. M. Dickey Drysdale, the editor of *The Herald of Randolph*, the weekly newspaper that serves the county, said he wasn't surprised by the outrage he was hearing that fall.

"We've gone over fifteen to twenty years from one of the more rural, conservative states in the country to one of the more liberal, and there have been a lot of people who have been hurt."

Sen. Jim Jeffords arrives in Vermont to announce that he is leaving the Republican Party.

"You know, I could never be a Democrat, but I could be an independent."

Chapter 7

Jim Jeffords: the Power of One

On September 12, 1972, Jim Jeffords suffered what would be his only defeat in a forty-year political career: He lost a race for the Republican nomination for governor in a bitter primary in which the GOP establishment worked for his opponent. In one radio interview a few weeks before the primary, Jeffords had said, "They're trying to force me out of the party." Now, at an election night party at the Little Valley House, a tavern just outside Montpelier, a group of Jeffords' supporters pulled him aside and offered him $5,000 to help finance a Jeffords bid as an independent. He declined. Yes, he admitted, he was mad at the party machine for taking a stand in a primary; yes, he was angry that Deane Davis, the popular retiring governor, had supported Jeffords' opponent even though Jeffords, as attorney general, had worked closely with Davis to push through the governor's pioneering proposals on environmental protection and water quality. Republicanism, though, was in Jeffords' blood and heritage; all of the men he admired growing up—George Aiken, Ernest Gibson, Leonard Wing—were Republican. It would take a great deal for him to turn his back on such a deeply rooted association.

The 1972 defeat was not the first time the GOP establishment had worked against him, however. In Jeffords' initial statewide race—for attorney general in 1968—he had faced Joseph Palmisano, the state's attorney for Washington County, in the Republican primary. Palmisano was a law-and-order conservative highly critical of the rulings on civil rights that were coming from the U.S. Supreme Court under the leadership of Chief Justice Earl Warren. Deane Davis, running then for his first term as governor, and other Republican leaders worked behind the scenes for Palmisano. Jeffords defeated Palmisano, nonetheless, and went on to victory in November, but the divisions festered.

As Jeffords conceded defeat at the Little Valley House in that 1972 primary, Joe Jamele stood at his side. Jamele was the campaign manager for Democratic nominee Tom Salmon. Democrats back then could already see that Jeffords' supporters were liberal and many of them were independents, so rather than spending primary night with Salmon, Jamele went to Jeffords' primary night headquarters to sign up as many of his supporters and campaign workers as possible. It was part of the Democrats' strategy to turn the GOP split into their advantage, and it worked. Tom Salmon was elected governor.

Two years later Jeffords ran for the U.S. House. The incumbent, Republican Dick Mallary, was running for the U.S. Senate seat held for 34 years by George Aiken, who was retiring. Jeffords again faced a difficult three-way primary, this time against Lt. Gov. Jack Burgess and Madeline Harwood, a state senator from Bennington County who served as the Republican National Committeewoman for Vermont. What made this primary especially tricky was that Burgess and Jeffords were expected to split the moderate/liberal vote, giving Harwood a clear shot at the conservative vote. "I wish to state that I am known as a conservative, and I expect to run a conservative campaign," she said in her announcement, hammering home her conviction by wearing a red, white and blue dress. In the end the race was close: Burgess garnered 11,453 votes, but Jeffords defeated Harwood 18,573-16,345. The general election was an easy win for Jeffords over former Burlington Mayor Frank Cain, but as evidence even then of his appeal among independent and Democratic voters, Jeffords was the sole Republican to win one of the top state offices. Democrat Pat Leahy defeated Mallary for the U.S. Senate, becoming the first Vermont Democrat ever to be elected to the Senate; Salmon won re-election as governor, and Democrats won the offices of lieutenant governor and attorney general. Besides Jeffords, the only Republicans to win statewide were the candidates for auditor and secretary of state.

My most vivid memory of this campaign is of Harwood's television ads. They were produced by the Robert Goodman Agency, in Baltimore, and included a song with the refrain "Someone to believe in; someone we

> Democrats back then could already see that Jeffords' supporters were liberal and many of them were independents, so [they worked]...to sign up as many of his supporters and campaign workers as possible.

can all join hands with." That fall I was still a student at Middlebury College, and I wrote a newspaper column for the Valley Voice bemoaning her big media campaign and use of an advertising agency to sell a candidate in Vermont. I cringe reading that column today: Her campaign was a low-key, personal effort; for much of its early part she drove herself around the state. In retrospect, the campaign ad played a small role, especially when compared with the sophisticated ad campaigns of today. It certainly didn't win her the primary. The other image I carry from that election is of Jeffords wearing a neck brace. In September he had been rear-ended at a stoplight and afterwards was forced to wear a big, white neck brace for the rest of the campaign. He was still wearing the brace when he arrived in Washington in

January, and he tells the story of walking into a reception for new House members with another freshman Republican who was on crutches. A Democrat, relishing the post-Watergate drubbing the Republicans endured, called out, "There's two we almost got."

Despite being a freshman in the minority party, Jeffords received plenty of national press upon his arrival in Washington. The congressman-elect, facing personal and campaign debt, decided to live in the RV travel camper that he had used to tour the state during the campaign. He rented a site behind a Holiday Inn in College Park, Maryland, and took a public bus back and forth to the Capitol. The unusual housing arrangement brought him notice on national television programs, and made him the subject of numerous articles and photos. Jeffords received another round of such publicity in 1981, when he gave up his apartment, which was being converted into a condominium, and moved into his House office to sleep on a pullout couch.

Over the years, though, Jeffords won attention for more than his quirky living arrangements. He gained a reputation as a person who did his homework and understood the inner workings of the legislative process, with his signature issues being agriculture, education and the environment. He gradually acquired the reputation of a maverick, both for his willingness to challenge the Republican leadership and for his involvement with an eclectic array of issues and people. One such example was his role in bringing Soviet dissidents to this country. His interest was sparked by an article he read in 1976 that said Alexandr Solzhensitsyn wanted to emigrate to the United States and was possibly interested in relocating to Vermont. Jeffords jumped on the mention of his state and somehow managed to get a letter, in Russian, to Solzhenitsyn, who replied that he would love to settle in the state. Jeffords remembers later sharing a bottle of excellent Russian vodka with the author on his first night in his new home.

Anyone looking for the seeds that would lead to Jeffords' 2001 decision to abandon the Republican Party would easily find them twenty years before—when Ronald Reagan became president. At issue were the budget and tax cuts that were at the heart of Reagan's agenda. The president courted a group of conservative Democrats who came to be known as the Boll Weevils. Jeffords decided to counter with a group of moderate Republicans who were dubbed the Gypsy Moths. The White House was furious, with one official dubbing their move a "counter-coup." That official directed his ire at Jeffords particularly, canceling a perk accorded every other member of the House, that of being able to give visiting constituents tour passes for the White House. Undaunted, Jeffords and the Gypsy Moths were able to win some changes in Reagan's proposal, enough so that in good conscience Jeffords could vote for Reagan's revised budget. But he opposed the president's three-year tax cut, the only Republican in the House to do so. The White House, eager to have unanimous GOP backing in the House, leveled its fury at Jeffords, as did many Vermont conservatives and other Reagan supporters in the state.

In 1988 Jeffords ran for the U.S. Senate seat that had been held since 1971 by Bob Stafford. Jeffords today may be a hero among the Democrats, but in each of his three Senate runs he faced strong Democratic opponents who argued that Jeffords was a nice guy and a moderate but he was still a Republican. They pointed out that he supported the Republican leadership and Republican positions. Jeffords countered that he always voted his conscience, regardless of party positions. In 1988 Jeffords defeated Burlington lawyer Bill Gray; in 1994 he won against state Sen. Jan Backus, and in 2000 he won his final term by defeating state Auditor Ed Flanagan.

Jeffords' presence in the Senate—pre-2001—was much like his presence in the House, quiet and unassuming. He avoided the Sunday talk shows and shied away from publicity. Instead, he concentrated his efforts in committees, where he continued to give the Republican leadership heartburn—for example, by opposing the 1991 nomination of

Clarence Thomas to the Supreme Court and later the GOP's 1994 Contract With America (he said it had "a southern, religious-right focus"). Later still, he looked like a turncoat for favoring President Clinton's 1993 healthcare reform proposal, the only Republican senator to serve as a co-sponsor. Clinton once famously called Jeffords his favorite Republican senator, although the president joked in 1998 that "I used to refer to Senator Jeffords as my favorite Republican, and then I was informed that I had endangered his committee chairmanship—and his physical well being—so I never do that anymore." Sen. Edward Kennedy, the liberal lion of the Senate, worked closely with Jeffords on health-care reform and even came to his assistance in Jeffords' 1994 re-election campaign, when Vermont Democrats condemned him as ineffective.

> **The whole visit reminded me that our elected officials have to grapple with the stresses and strains of their private lives while they live on a very public stage. This was especially true with Jeffords....**

His uneasy relationship with the conservatives, who were growing in number and strength, was most evident in 1997, when Jeffords was in line to chair the Labor, Health, and Human Resources Committee, later renamed the Health, Education, Labor, and Pension Committee. Conservatives wanted Sen. Dan Coats, of Indiana, to get the post over Jeffords, even though Coats was junior to Jeffords. In the end, Sen. Trent Lott, the majority leader, decided not to jettison the seniority system for deciding committee chairs and urged the caucus to choose Jeffords. However, the mere fact that Jeffords had to beg and fight for something that should have been his without question was more evidence that the Republican Party was not a comfortable home for Vermont's junior senator.

The tension between Jeffords and the Republicans flared up again during the Clinton impeachment. Those difficult months revealed the agony Jeffords endured as he wrestled with tough decisions: He awoke with nightmares, drenched in sweat, as the impeachment proceeded. Jeffords felt strongly that Clinton had let him down, but he also believed that the president's wrongdoing—lying about something that was not a crime—did not rise to the level of high crimes and misdemeanors that required his removal from office. Jeffords walked a fine line, voting with the Republicans on early procedural motions but voting in the end to acquit.

I saw Jeffords in Washington when I went down to cover the end of the impeachment trial in the Senate and to report on the roles Jeffords and Leahy were playing in the trial. His appearance shocked me; he looked as if he had aged ten years in the couple of months since I had seen him. Erik Smulson, Jeffords' communications director, told me that the senator's back and neck problems, worsened by a second and more serious car accident, this one in Washington in 1997, were really bothering him and that he was taking a pain medication that affected his focus. Meanwhile, Jeffords' wife, Liz, who had been battling cancer and who had suffered a heart attack in 1998, was continuing to have her own health problems. One night I left Jeffords' office as he was getting ready to leave. At the time he was being shadowed by a team from NBC's "Dateline" program, which was doing a segment on the pressure Jeffords faced on the impeachment vote. The next morning I talked to Smulson and learned that after I had left, Jeffords, some members of his staff and the "Dateline" crew had been trapped in a tiny Capitol elevator that got stuck between two floors after it shot up a few floors and then dropped back. They were in the elevator until close to midnight.

The whole visit reminded me that our elected officials have to grapple with the stresses and strains of their private lives while they live on a very public stage. This was especially true with Jeffords, whose 1978 divorce from his wife, Liz, was very public, as was the reconciliation that led them to remarry in 1986.

At the end of 1999 I was back in Washington to watch Jeffords try to renew the Northeast Interstate Dairy Compact. Jeffords' office became the command center in what turned out to be the most contentious issue in the closing weeks of the congressional session. Before it was over, the ranking Democrat on the House Appropriations Committee had tied up the House in procedural votes in an effort to kill the compact. Senate opponents threatened to shut down the entire federal government and filibustered to block action on a $390 billion budget bill. Jeffords' heart was in the compact because he knew it would be a lifesaver for New England dairy farmers, but he also knew this innovative idea was home-grown in Vermont. Almost a decade earlier, when then-state Rep. Bobby Starr, of North Troy, had wondered if there was anything the states could do to boost milk prices, Dan Smith, then a legislative draftsman for the Legislature, had come up with the idea of an interstate compact that would set minimums paid to farmers for fluid milk produced within a region.

Back then no one was optimistic the compact could be enacted because it would require votes of endorsement by both chambers in each legislature in all six New England states. After that, Congress would have to approve it. The hardest part turned out to be getting that Congressional approval. The compact died in Congress in 1994, but was re-introduced in 1995. Proponents managed to put the measure into the 1996 farm bill, only to have it stripped out by a Senate vote of 50-46. However, the chairman of the Senate Agriculture Committee, Sen. Richard Lugar, endorsed the compact during his brief presidential bid, and in a bipartisan show of raw political power he and Leahy added the compact back into the farm bill at the final moment and rammed it through.

In 1999 proponents worked hard to win reauthorization, but opponents, primarily dairy processors and Midwestern legislators, blocked passage through the normal legislative process. In the end it came down to Jeffords, who was then a Republican and thus a member of the majority party. Gov. Howard Dean, speaking of Jeffords, had put it bluntly at a September news conference: "At the end of the day you have to deliver the bacon."

Jeffords did. He worked closely with Leahy and with Rep. Bernie Sanders, but in the end he put his clout on the line. He did it the old-fashioned way, with some adroit deal making and unending persistence. Day after day he was the squeaky wheel. Rep. Nancy Johnson, R-Conn., told me, "Senator Jeffords was the key. Make no mistake about it. He wielded his power on this issue. In the end, we got a very good deal over enormous opposition." This victory on the compact was probably the biggest factor in Sanders' decision not to challenge Jeffords' re-election in 2000. It would have been hard to attack Jeffords as ineffective when he had delivered this most important boost to the state's farmers. However, the compact's victory, in which GOP leader Trent Lott had come to Jeffords' assistance, would haunt him. In 2001 Jeffords' defection infuriated Lott and other Senate Republicans, who felt he was abandoning them after they had supported one of his most heartfelt pieces of legislation.

In 2001, just a few months into the new Bush administration, Jeffords voted against President George W. Bush's $1.6 trillion tax cut. The White House, seeking to punish Jeffords, quickly zeroed in on the dairy compact as the vehicle for revenge. In a city where nothing happens by chance, a series of articles popped up in various publications in early May 2001 signaling that the White House was considering burying the dairy compact to punish Jeffords. "White House weighs action vs. Jeffords; Tax Rebellion by Jeffords Sours Dairy Compact," read the headline and subheadline in *The Hill*, a publication for Congress insiders. *The Weekly Standard*, a conservative newspaper, headlined its article: "James Jeffords (R-Sort of): Revenge is a dish best served with milk." The theme of the articles was best summed up by this quotation from an anonymous senior GOP source: "The White House is not giving specifics, but there's a one- or two-year plan to punish him for his behavior. And it's stuff that may hurt him, but stuff that's not going to draw a significant amount of attention. So they're going to get him." *The Weekly Standard* was the most specific, predicting that the "most likely retribution" would be for the GOP to kill the dairy compact. "What better way to punish Jeffords than by denying him his pet project and doing away with a prime example of pork?" To Vermonters, however, the dairy compact was anything but pork. It was a critical program crucial to the survival of Vermont's dwindling numbers of farms.

We would learn after the fact that it was in this period that Jeffords began seriously thinking about leaving the Republican Party. He mentioned the prospect for the first time on March 30, when he met with Sen. Chris Dodd, a Democrat from Connecticut. As the two talked about funding for special education, Jeffords' frustrations spilled out: He complained that despite being chairman of the Senate committee on education, he was battling both the White House and his own party over providing education aid for those with disabilities. In a time of huge surpluses and so many unmet needs, he asked, why was everyone in his party deaf to those needs and so eager to give tax breaks to the wealthy?

According to Jeffords, Dodd told him, "You know, Jim, there is always room over here with us."

A long silence followed.

Finally, Jeffords spoke: "You know, I could never be a Democrat, but I could be an independent."

Those close to Jeffords differ on when the senator actually decided to shed his Republican label. His closest aide at the time, Susan Boardman Russ, says she believes Jeffords came to the realization on May 15 when he met with the Senate Democratic leaders to formally discuss a switch. His wife, Liz, says the final decision came a week later, on the 22nd, when Jeffords appeased the reservations of his conservative son. Jeffords, himself, says it was the next day, as he flew back to

Vermont following an emotional meeting with his moderate GOP colleagues. But everyone agrees there were several key moments in the path to independence, and none was more important than Wednesday, April 4, just five days after Jeffords' comments to Dodd.

Not by coincidence I received a telephone call that morning at around 9:30 from Andrew Card, the White House chief of staff. He clearly intended to use me both to get a message to Jeffords and to ensure that Vermonters knew that their junior senator was the sole obstacle to passage of the president's top priority. I was stunned, but of course flattered, that the White House chief of staff was calling.

Card was from Massachusetts and had served in the Massachusetts House. There was some talk that he wanted to run for governor there someday, so we chatted about New England politics, and I seem to remember him saying he had been in Maine the past weekend. Then came the hard sell. He asked that Jeffords "give the president a chance." The budget vote, he said, was a crucial

> In a dramatic moment Jeffords walked into a news conference being held by Sen. John Breaux, D-La., and said he would join what was being called the Centrist Coalition in opposing the Bush tax cut.

moment in the new Bush presidency and was more symbolic than substantive. Jeffords, I knew, had been protesting that the $1.6 trillion tax cut was too much; he wanted a lower tax cut and he wanted a firm commitment from the administration to add $180 billion to special education over the next ten years. Jeffords' goal was for the federal government to finally honor the commitment it had made in 1975 to pay forty percent of the costs of special education. His specific plan was to transform the Individuals with Disabilities Education Act, known as IDEA, from a discretionary program that must compete for funds every year to a program with a mandatory appropriation. That act requires states to make special provisions for students with disabilities, many of which are quite expensive, but the U.S. has paid only a tiny fraction of those costs. Vermont, as a rural state with many small schools, has been hit especially hard by those costs.

I asked Card about Jeffords' proposal, and he responded that it would be a mistake to make the program an entitlement. Throwing more smoke than substance in my face, he said such a change would preclude any efforts at reforming the program and that furthermore, education reform was a high priority for Bush. Later that day when I read Card's quotation to Jeffords, he was apoplectic. He retorted that special education was already a federal mandate, and all he wanted was for the federal government to meet its commitment to pay its share of the cost. This had nothing to do with reform, and he would welcome education reform proposals, he said.

As it turned out, Andy Card's hard sell on me was wasted effort. By that afternoon Jeffords' patience with the White House's effort to buy time ran out. In a dramatic moment Jeffords walked into a news conference being held by Sen. John Breaux, D-La., and said he would join what was being called the Centrist Coalition in opposing the Bush tax cut. Two days later, on Friday, Jeffords voted for a $1.25 trillion tax cut. Late that day I interviewed Jeffords on "Vermont This Week," the public affairs program I host on Vermont Public Television. I asked him if he expected any reprisals for breaking with the president. He said he doubted it because they know that "It is a short walk across the aisle." That statement generated much speculation in Washington and in Vermont that Jeffords was threatening to bolt the party. I discounted it, though, because in a 50-50 Senate, Jeffords' vote would be crucial on most every roll call.

A month later, however, the House and Senate conference committee reached agreement on a tax cut of $1.35 trillion. Gone was the extra money for education Jeffords had fought for. On Thursday, May 10, he voted against the budget, saying, "I cannot hide my disappointment that the Congress once again will not fulfill its pledge to fully fund special education."

The next day I wrote about the articles and editorials that were appearing in Washington publications. They quoted anonymous Republican sources saying that the White House was preparing a plan to get back at Jeffords. I focused on the political reality that it just did not make any sense for the White House to attack Jeffords: "On revenge, the simple truth is that Bush and Cheney need Jeffords more than Jeffords needs them. He is the chairman of the Senate committee that controls Bush's top priority of education. In a 50-50 Senate his vote will be needed time after time."

Events moved quickly, though. Four days later Jeffords met at 8 a.m. in his private Capitol office with Democratic leaders Tom Daschle and Harry Reid. They seriously discussed the possibility of Jeffords switching to an independent. The following day Erik Smulson, Jeffords' chief spokesman, hinted at the switch by saying that "regardless of party label [Jeffords] will do what he thinks is right for Vermont and the nation." This was a far cry from Smulson's reassuring comment the previous month that "Senator Jeffords is a Republican and he expects to be a Republican the rest of his life." I caught the change in Smulson's answer and began calling sources in Vermont and Washington to help me interpret the shift in language. While it was becoming clear that Jeffords was considering becoming an independent, I could not determine if a decision had already been made. Part of the difficulty was that Jeffords himself was not ready to cut off his ties with his longtime moderate friends in the Senate, and thus was sending them conflicting signals. By Tuesday the 22nd, though, sources were saying that all that stood between Jeffords and the switch was a conversation with his son, Leonard.

Once that was completed, the only question remaining was whether the decision would be announced in Washington or Vermont. Jeffords chose Vermont. On Thursday, May 24, at 9:30 a.m., the senator walked into a conference room of a Burlington hotel where a crowded press conference was being beamed live on national television. He spoke simply and from the heart: "In order to best represent my state of Vermont, my own conscience and principles that I have stood for my whole life, I will leave the Republican Party and become an independent."

Twice in that news conference I saw tears in Jeffords' eyes, once when supporters began chanting their thanks and later when he discussed the pain his decision would bring to his GOP colleagues. "My colleagues, many of them my friends for years, may find it difficult in their hearts to befriend me any longer," he said. "Many of my supporters will be disappointed and some of my staffers will see their lives upended. I regret this very much."

> He walked out of his office holding a copy of the June 4 edition of Newsweek with his photo on the cover and the headline "Mr. Jeffords Blows up Washington." He grinned and asked, "Can you believe it?"

Immediately after making his announcement, Jeffords flew to Italy via Washington to attend a conference on environmental issues. He delayed the effective date of his decision to become an independent to the close of business on June 5 to allow for an orderly transition in what would be the first change in partisan control of the U.S. Senate outside an election. Although an independent, Jeffords would caucus with the Democrats on organizational matters, which meant they would have a majority in the Senate. On Monday, June 4, I flew down to Washington to be there to cover the switch in power. I arrived late in the day, expecting to see only Erik Smulson, but Jeffords had waited for me. He walked out of his office holding a copy of the June 4 edition of *Newsweek* with his photo on the cover and the headline "Mr. Jeffords Blows up Washington." He grinned and asked, "Can you believe it?" Throughout the office were signs of the seismic shift Jeffords had caused. Flowers filled the reception area, and interns and staff members were sorting boxes of mail piled in conference rooms into those messages supporting Jeffords' decision and those opposing it. As a further sign of the tumult he had unleashed, a team of Capitol police provided security in light of death threats against the senator.

Jeffords told me that evening that he had no regrets and felt increasingly confident that he had done the right thing. He said the worldwide reaction had overwhelmed him, "the feeling that I had done something that might literally save the country from very difficult problems." He said he was deeply hurt, though, by the reaction of outgoing Majority Leader Trent Lott, who called Jeffords' action "a coup of one" and "the impetuous decision of one man to undermine our democracy."

"I thought we were pretty good friends," said Jeffords.

Technically, Jeffords became an independent with the fall of the final gavel Tuesday afternoon. Symbolically, however, he took the step earlier in the day when he walked into the Lyndon B. Johnson Room, where the Democrats held their weekly lunches. As Jeffords opened the door and entered the room with its giant windows overlooking the east lawn of the Capitol, the senators stood and applauded for several minutes. Following the lunch, Jeffords left the Capitol to join other senators at a meeting with President Bush on education issues. Dozens of reporters and photographers swarmed Jeffords on the marble steps as he left the building; crowds of tourists visiting the Capitol waited as well. When he appeared at the top of the stairs the tourists broke into applause and cheers. "I am so glad that someone stood up for his integrity and did what he did," said James Randall, of California, a tourist who was standing next to me. "This is the highlight of my trip."

On Wednesday, June 6, 2001, shortly after noon, Jim Jeffords entered the Senate chamber to cast his first vote as an independent. He announced his vote to the clerk and then moved down the center aisle to the third row to check out his new seat on the Democratic side. The desk had been moved from the Republican side earlier in the day. He walked along the crescent of desks, stopping at each one, until he found his own. He sat down, looked up at me in the press gallery, grinned and gave me a thumbs up.

Later that day Jeffords met with a group of schoolchildren from Williston. Paul Alexander, a writer for *Rolling Stone*, and I accompanied him from the Hart Building through the bowels of the Capitol. Two burly guards flanked Jeffords. As tourists, congressional staffers and others recognized him, they started applauding and cheering. Some reached out for him, as if he were a rock star. I followed and found it hard to grasp that this was Jim Jeffords, the ah-shucks Vermonter who shunned publicity. Paul then tugged on my arm and pointed at Jeffords' shoes. "His shoe lace is untied," he said. "Should we tell the guards?"

At the end of that historic day Jeffords and I sat down together in the television recording studio in the Senate basement. I was getting the first one-on-one interview with Jeffords since the switch; the interview would be broadcast Friday on "Vermont This Week," and the transcript would run on the AP wire. In keeping with the senator's practice all week, he was giving interviews only to the Vermont media. So as we did our interview, David Rosenbaum, of *The New York Times*, sat nearby taking notes. Jeffords said he felt he had accomplished what he set out to do: "I believe the message has been delivered to the White House that they need to meet with both sides of the aisle to get things accomplished."

History books a century from now will include a mention of Jeffords' switch; presidential scholars will write about and hold symposiums on how Bush mishandled Jeffords and the consequences. Here in Vermont, Jeffords will be noted as the last of the top elected officials to come from that era when everyone was Republican. But he could not stay the course. In the span of forty years Jeffords did not change, but his party did, as the more liberal members found a new home in the Democratic Party. For me, though, the Jeffords legacy is wrapped up in his unending optimism, his conviction that he could make the world a better place. He went to Washington much like the character Jefferson Smith in *Mr. Smith Goes to Washington*, and remarkably, he maintained that idealism and optimism throughout his entire career. The President and White House staff had heard all the rumors that Jeffords might switch parties, but no one thought them credible because they doubted any senator would make such a bold move. Jeffords proved them wrong and showed the nation the power of one.

Presidential candidate Howard Dean wades into a crowd of supporters at a 2003 rally in Boston.

"I'm Howard Dean, and I'm here to represent the Democratic wing of the Democratic Party."

Chapter 8

Dean for America

Howard Dean's call came unexpectedly on a Saturday night during the New Year's holiday. He called me at home to say he was abandoning his bid for president. The date was January 3, 1998; he had intended to be a contender in the 2000 presidential election. At that time most people were unaware that Dean was actively campaigning for the presidency, but those of us in the Vermont media were not only well aware but probably a bit obsessed by it. Dean had been inching toward a bid for much of 1997, traveling extensively as chairman of the Democratic Governors Association, touching bases with all the right people. His was a long shot, but there was no doubt he was being taken seriously. At the California state Democratic convention, he had brought 3,000 delegates to their feet, roaring their approval of his prescription for conservative finances, moderate social stands and a strong dose of helping children.

Then he got rolled by Al Gore. It wasn't pretty, and it showed starkly that Dean wasn't ready for prime time. In early December 1997 Dean and his top political adviser, Bob Rogan, stopped by Gore's White House office to let the vice president know as a courtesy that Dean was strongly inclined to run for president. Dean did not expect the meeting to become public, but it quickly did; within hours Gore had told President Clinton, and word began spreading around Washington and back to Vermont. In the Gore-Clinton version, Dean had told Gore he was planning to run regardless of whether Gore did. Dean found the ensuing publicity especially awkward because he had been telling Vermonters that he would not make any decision on a 2000 presidential run for at least another year, until sometime after the 1998 elections. At a news conference only the day before he visited Gore, Dean had responded angrily to the continued peppering of questions from the State House press on whether he would run for president. "I'm not going to play the game anymore," he had declared, hoping to end the annoying speculation. However, when reporters learned that within 48 hours he had subsequently flown to Washington to tell Gore of his plans, the press corps had a good romp and Vermonters lost no time voicing their disapproval.

A poll by news organizations conducted in December 1997 showed that Vermonters strongly disapproved of Dean pursuing the presidency while he remained governor. They felt he should stay put in the state and attend to the issues they had elected him to resolve. Dean was so surprised by the results that he conducted his own polling, but the numbers were similar, prompting him to move up his timetable for decision-making.

In Burlington he sat down with his family over the holidays, and his wife and two children told him in no uncertain terms that they did not want him traveling the country for the next two years. With the decision made, he called me that Saturday to get the news out, saying that he wanted to put the second-guessing behind him before the start of the 1998 legislative session the following Tuesday. "Your children are only in high school and middle school once," he explained. When we hung up, I went into the office and wrote that Dean would not seek the presidency in 2000. Like most political observers, I considered Dean's presidential aspirations to be over. Rogan, who had been coordinating the presidential campaign, left Dean's staff and went into the private sector. Dean ran and won another term as governor in 1998, and then another term in 2000, both hard-fought campaigns that kept him focused on the state as he defended the passage of Act 60, a radical overhaul of state education financing, and civil unions, then coped with the fiery aftermath of both.

In September 2001, a week before 9/11, Dean announced that he would not run for governor in 2002. There was some talk at that news conference about whether he might run for president in 2004, but I discounted it. I felt that because he had promoted and signed the civil unions law, he was unelectable. I imagined Karl Rove, Bush's political adviser, having a field day running negative ads about Dean and civil unions, much the way Bush's father and Lee Atwater had destroyed Mike Dukakis with the Willie Horton ad in the 1988 presidential campaign. I wasn't alone in that sentiment. In August of 2003 as Bill Clinton tried to stop Dean's rise by building support for Wes Clark's bid for the presidency, Clinton reportedly said, "Howard Dean forfeited his right to run for president when he signed the civil unions bill. He can't win."

Dean saw things differently, however. On Monday, November 19, 2001, fourteen months before he would leave his eleven-year stint as Vermont's governor, he called me to say that he was forming a federal political action committee—"The Fund for a Healthy America"—to finance his political travels and to contribute to Democratic campaigns around the country. He said he had not yet made up his mind whether to take a second run at the presidency, but he would do so after he left the governor's office in January 2003. In the meantime his PAC would promote his signature issues: "fiscal stability, universal healthcare and equal rights for all Americans." In May of 2002, though, his intentions became clearer when he formed "Dean for America" to serve as the formal vehicle for his presidential campaign.

What quickly became evident as Dean emerged as a presidential candidate was how little we knew about him as a person, despite how long he had served in the state's top position. That's simply how it is in Vermont: Governors are public officials but still private individuals. They live in their own homes, their spouses need not make any public appearances and their children are off limits to the press unless one of them gets into a legal jam. And while such privacy is a Vermont tradition, Dean carried it further than most. As governor he tended to be remote and private, his behavior probably stemming in part from his background as a doctor, many of whom focus on the immediate problem at hand, solve it and move on, keeping the world an arm's length away. Only once in his nearly twelve years in office do I remember Dean losing his reserve in public. At a 1997 news conference he choked up as he discussed his strong feelings about the state police. He was incensed that a published report might have given troopers the feeling he wasn't 1,000 percent behind them. "You really struck a nerve because I am so pro-law enforcement," said Dean. He paused, bowed his head, blinked, cleared his throat and fought to keep his composure. "I think of some of the funerals I've been to . . . some of the troopers who have lost their lives. . . . This is something I feel strongly about."

Now, though, the demands of a presidential campaign required that Dean open up his life—and I played key roles in the two biggest steps he took to do so. The first came in February of 2002. Sue Allen, who had worked for me at the AP but who was now Dean's press secretary, tracked me down on a Friday afternoon as I headed to Colchester to do my weekly television show on Vermont Public Television. She asked if I could be available to drop by the governor's house in Burlington that evening. She said he had something he wanted to give me to read over the weekend. This was very mysterious and very unlike Dean. Although

I had been to several governors' homes over the years, I had never been to Dean's, and I had never received a similar call. When I stopped by the governor's house in the evening, he gave me a well-worn, legal-sized, expandable brown file, held together with string. The bottom corners were torn, a sign of its use, its importance and its travels. Its precious contents, I learned, were the pieces of a puzzle that Dean and his family had worked on for 27 years, namely, the mysterious disappearance of Dean's brother, Charlie, a young adventurer who at 24 had set off to travel around the world, who had been taken a prisoner of war in Laos and who subsequently had been killed.

The governor had never publicly told his brother's story. We all knew that he wore Charlie's belt every day in memory of his brother—even though the big black belt didn't fit very well and often did not go with what Dean was wearing—but we knew nothing of the story. In the past he had declined to talk about it, although he made vague references at meetings with relatives of

> What quickly became evident as Dean emerged as a presidential candidate was how little we knew about him as a person, despite how long he had served in the state's top position.

POW-MIAs of understanding their pain. The rumor among the press corps was that Charlie had been with the CIA and had been taken prisoner in Laos. I took the file home and spent the weekend reading the hundreds of documents and piecing together the frenzied effort in 1974 by the U.S. government and the Dean family, first to determine what had happened to Charlie and then to win his release. "We now consider it almost certain that Charles Dean is the person under Pathet Lao detention," reads an urgent teletype message sent from Laos to the Department of Defense National Military Command Center.

"In light of evident Pathet Lao suspicion that Dean and [traveling companion Neil] Sharman are intelligence agents, our texts will stress that Dean is a recent university graduate and ordinary tourist. In delivering these communications, we will impress upon addressees the seriousness with which we view Dean's detention."

The teletype is signed simply "WHITEHOUSE," for Charles S. Whitehouse, then U.S. ambassador to Laos. For Whitehouse the case was personal; he and Charlie Dean's father had been classmates at Yale.

The Dean family worked hard to win Charlie's release. Dean's father, who was also named Howard Dean (the two were referred to within the family as Big Howard and Little Howard), visited the State Department and Capitol Hill, then traveled to Laos in December of 1974. The elder Mrs. Dean visited there in February of 1975. Word came in November from two Laotians who had escaped from Pathet Lao detention that Dean and Sharman were alive. Later Dean and Sharman managed to get photos of themselves smuggled to U.S. officials by a Lao who had been detained with them. Sometime in March or April of 1975, though, Howard Dean the father learned through unofficial channels that his son had been killed by his captors. Later information indicated that the Pathet Lao had shot and killed both Dean and Sharman on December 14, 1974.

After reading through the material, I met the following week with Dean in his fifth floor penthouse in the Pavilion Office Building. Slowly the story came out: how the family had had a memorial service for Charlie in May of 1975 in East Hampton, New York; how Charlie had been the born politician, the president of his class in boarding school, a political activist at the University of North Carolina and a field worker for the 1972 presidential campaign of George McGovern in both New York and North Carolina. Dean spoke to me of how painful it was for the family, especially his father, that so many unanswered questions remained, and how hard it was to accept that his brother's remains were still halfway around the world in an unknown grave.

When Dean became lieutenant governor in 1987, U.S. Sen. Patrick Leahy arranged a Pentagon briefing on his brother's case. Dean made requests under the Freedom of Information Act. More and more information filled the expandable file: reports from informants in Laos; photos from aerial reconnaissance; declassified intelligence reports. Over the years the family pieced together much of the puzzle. Charlie, who had left New York in the spring of 1973 to drive to Seattle, had then sailed to Japan on a freighter and traveled on to Bali and Australia, where he worked on a ranch for nine months. After that experience, he went to Laos, where on September 4, 1974, he and Sharman had been detained at a checkpoint, probably because they carried cameras and were thus thought to be spies.

As Dean walked me through the documents and filled out the time-line for me, he was surprisingly dispassionate, as if the subject were the state budget for the coming year. When I questioned him about Charlie as a person, however, Dean's composure crumpled. He choked back tears and then cried as he explained that Charlie — not he—was sup-posed to have been the politician. He talked about Charlie's time in North Carolina and how he dominated every room he entered. Dean said he was talking about Charlie now, after all the years of silence, because a new effort by the Defense Department's Joint Task Force Full Accounting had turned up the most reliable information to date: that Charlie and Sharman had been taken by truck and killed a few miles shy of the Vietnamese border.

Now, Dean told me, he was going to travel to that site the follow-ing week. He did so, and called me just after helicoptering to the site, describing in emotional terms what it was like to finally be there. He also talked at length about the importance of the excavation projects as a way to help members of his family and others like them who had spent so many decades wondering what had happened to their loved ones.

Over the course of the presidential campaign I was fascinated to see Dean open up and start to tell his personal story to national reporters in a way he had never done in Vermont. He had no other choice.

Candidates for president are expected to provide a compelling narrative—whether it is Bill Clinton's "Man from Hope" or George W. Bush's victory over alcoholism—while we in Vermont have never required that of our candidates for governor. As governor, though, Dean had consciously walled off his personal background in ways other governors had not—even by Vermont standards. We all knew of Dick Snelling's bankruptcy and Madeleine Kunin's immigrant story, but Dean had never let us see more than the doctor-politician angle. I suspect he may have been concerned that his background of New York wealth and summers in the Hamptons would not have played well in the rural pockets of Vermont, but I think he would have been far more prepared for the national scrutiny of his personal story if he had started telling it to us years before.

We would learn much more about Dean and his feelings about Charlie's death in the coming year. In mid-November the Defense Department announced that Charlie's remains had finally been found, although at a different location than the one Dean had visited in February. This led to another round of news stories, and now that Dean was the apparent frontrunner for the Democratic nomination, the questions were more direct and the answers necessarily deeper. Dean told several reporters traveling with him that he had been in therapy in the early 1980s because of anxiety attacks that appeared to be related to his grief over his brother's death. He imprecisely told a reporter for the *Washington Post* that he had suffered panic attacks, but then quickly explained that the attacks more closely resembled run-of-the-mill anxiety. Nonetheless, the reporter called them panic attacks in his story, and that angered Dean. It may have been because he was well aware how the press can distort or exploit a politician's displays of emotion. He had only to recall how Sen. Edmund Muskie's tears in 1972 as he defended his wife in New Hampshire had cost him his presidential bid.

The other major step Dean took to open up his life was to invite me to have a one-on-one interview with his wife, Judy. A year had passed since he had given me the information on Charlie. That it was a big deal to land an interview with the candidate's wife says much about Vermont and about Dean. He has always been fiercely protective of his family's privacy. "I think the traditional feeling among politicians is that they have to use their families as props or as appendages," he said. "My kids and my wife are very independent." Several times over the years he had criticized news organizations for reporting on incidents involving children of politicians, once even coming to the defense of George W. Bush. "I don't think it was proper of the press to print all that stuff about the twins' drinking," he said, speaking of Bush daughters Barbara and Jenna. "Those girls are just girls, and the only reason they got their names in the paper is because they are daughters of the president of the United States."

> The national press could not believe that Dean had been governor for almost twelve years and no reporter in Vermont had yet interviewed or profiled Judy Dean.

Judy Dean may have given one interview soon after her husband became governor, but she had given none since. She appeared publicly only to attend election night victory parties and inaugurations. The national press could not believe that Dean had been governor for almost twelve years and no reporter in Vermont had yet interviewed or profiled Judy Dean. They were equally shocked that no member of the Vermont press corps had demanded that we be allowed to see her. Now Dean's campaign had outgrown the state, however, and the rules were changing; the national press was beginning to grumble that it wasn't seeing Judy Dean in New Hampshire or in Iowa. Many wondered, frankly, why that was. Not surprisingly, rumors grew wildly in this vacuum. I received calls from political reporters asking whether the Deans were divorcing or if they were hiding some marital trouble.

Some political reporters claimed Dean didn't have a chance of winning the presidency if his wife was not at his side on the campaign trail.

Dean heard all of the criticism, but he remained firm that Judy would not be pulled into the campaign. "She's a doctor," Dean told me. "I can't imagine she is going to stop her practice to be going to Iowa or New Hampshire." I was never quite sure whether Dean was adamant about keeping his wife out of politics because she felt that way or because he thought she felt that way. Now, though, the campaign was facing enough questions about the "mystery wife" that she had agreed to do some interviews, starting with me. I suspect I was chosen because Judy knew me, and the campaign felt I would write a fair story, while I think the Deans feared the Washington press would steamroll her and paint her as an eccentric. But I had met Judy only once or perhaps twice while Dean was governor—I remember once was at his 1997 inauguration when we chatted for a few minutes—so I did not know her well. For this interview we met at her doctor's office in Shelburne, and I found her to be shy, which I expected, but also engaging and extremely down to earth. She grew animated when talking about her medical practice and her family, but was cautious when the conversation turned to herself and her role in the Dean presidential campaign.

What emerged, though, was a picture of why the Deans led, and continue to lead, such separate professional lives. They met in medical school while doing crossword puzzles in class. Dean came to Vermont for his residency in 1978, and Judy followed when she graduated a year later. The two married in 1981, the year Dean opened his medical practice in Shelburne with another doctor, and Judy joined the practice in 1985 after a fellowship at Montreal's McGill University.

Dean's slide into politics happened slowly, but it picked up momentum. He was a volunteer for Jimmy Carter's 1980 re-election campaign and then won election to the Vermont House in 1982. In 1986 he won election as lieutenant governor, but even that position is part time so he continued his medical practice. It wasn't until Snelling's sudden death in 1991 that Dean became a fulltime politician and gave up being a practicing doctor. "When she married me, she didn't know I was going to run for president of the United States. I didn't either. She married a doctor," Dean said, intimating that his wife might not have signed on to a marriage that required her to be a public person.

In that interview Judy Dean's apparent and, I thought, unrealistic belief that she would continue to practice medicine if Dean became president startled me. "I hope so, in some way, some how," she told me. Her husband was more blunt when I asked him: "If I win, Judy will practice medicine in Washington. That doesn't mean she will never go to a State dinner, but I don't see her job as entertainer." As for campaigning, Judy said she would not be unwilling to help him, but they had agreed she would not devote herself to his quest. "If he really wants me someplace, I certainly would do it, but it would be between me and him," she said.

Ironically, after the collapse of Dean's presidential campaign, he said one of his regrets was that he had not asked Judy to campaign with him sooner than the appearances she made in Iowa and New Hampshire. "She was a huge hit," he admitted. "We got all these wonderful letters afterwards saying it was so wonderful to see a normal person just like me in this role. I was shocked by how well she did, and I was more shocked that she liked it. She was great!"

On February 21, 2003, Dean stood before the winter meeting of the Democratic National Committee in Washington and started his speech with a series of bold questions: "What I want to know is why in the world the Democratic Party leadership is supporting the president's unilateral attack on Iraq! What I want to know is why are Democratic Party leaders supporting tax cuts! The question is not how big the tax cut should be! The question should be, 'Can we afford a tax cut at all with the largest deficit in the history of this country?'" He ran down a list of several other rather pointed questions and ended with,

"I'm Howard Dean, and I'm here to represent the Democratic wing of the Democratic Party." The crowd went wild, and the campaign started its climb.

A few weeks later I covered a Dean speech in Concord, New Hampshire. The campaign expected an audience of roughly 80 to 100 but more than 350 supporters and undecideds turned out. In listening to the tape of that event more than three years later, I almost laugh to hear Dean trying to explain what was then just starting on the Internet, namely, efforts to bring like-minded people together using an organization called Meetup. "Let me tell you what's been happening in our campaign, having nothing to do with us," he said, speaking to a crowd of supporters whose technological understanding of the Internet's possibilities no doubt ranged from the already converted to the completely baffled. "There is something called Meetup.org. I hardly know what it is. But they have these meetups, these Howard Dean meetups, and I went to one in New York, and there were 550 people in a place that only holds 250. A guy gave me a check for $5,000 for the campaign, on the spot. I had no idea who he was."

> This was the beginning of Howard Dean the "rock star," and it was utterly foreign to those of us who had covered him in Vermont while he fought for balanced budgets, stumbled through speeches and maintained decorum without a hint of passion.

Dean paused while his voice shifted from amazed to serious. "There is something going on in this country." From then, with each sentence, his voice grew louder just to be heard above the cheers and clapping. "People desperately want someone to stand up for American values. They are tired of being told by the right-wing talk show hosts and fundamental preachers how to live their lives. They desperately want their country back. We are going to take the country back, and you are going to take this country back. You are going to get on the Internet, you are going to talk to your friends, you are going to work hard. We are going to stand up for American values, and we are going to represent the Democratic wing of the Democratic party!"

I had never seen anything like it in almost twelve years of covering Dean in Vermont. This was the beginning of Howard Dean the "rock star," and it was utterly foreign to those of us who had covered him in Vermont while he fought for balanced budgets, stumbled through speeches and maintained decorum without a hint of passion. As governor he had been the detached doctor, figuring out what needed to be done and then doing it. As governor he always had his pulse on what the business community wanted and never lost sight of its needs. Running for president, he was becoming the spokesman for the forgotten man; he was becoming Bernie Sanders—and it was hard to comprehend.

Two weeks after that I traveled with Dean through a series of appearances he made in New York City. Speaking to The Women's Leadership Forum of the Democratic National Committee, he drew enthusiastic applause and cheers as he predicted the party was doomed to defeat unless it clearly defined its differences with the Republicans: "Bill Clinton said about four months ago that the American people will always vote for someone who is strong and wrong before they will vote for someone who is weak and right. We appear to be weak and right because we will say whatever it takes to win. And once you are willing to say whatever it takes to win, you lose."

Later that evening Dean spoke to a group of one hundred or so young professionals crowded into Mod, a trendy Upper West Side bar lounge. The audience was a tough sell, and Dean's early applause lines failed to generate any reaction. Four minutes into Dean's speech, however, the crowd came alive as he started talking about the economy and the president's tax cuts. The clamor of clapping and whistling filled the air as Dean noted his opposition to the war in Iraq: "I didn't support the president in Iraq, and I am not ashamed. We are not obligated to support the president's policy because this is not Iraq. This is the United States of America, and dissent is patriotic." Side conversations and the clinking of glasses stopped as Dean picked up the tempo. Now, as in New Hampshire, the hoots, whistles and cheers from the excited audience drowned out Dean's message as he launched into his closing: "I want our country back! I want our country back! I want to be proud again!"

By the time Dean formally launched his campaign, on June 23, I was no longer covering it. My son, Garrett, who had just graduated from college, had gone to work for the campaign in Burlington in the press office. Garrett had gotten to know Dean when he was a sophomore in high school participating in a community-based learning program. He started out doing clips and paperwork in the governor's press office, but his responsibilities increased over the next two years as the work caught his interest. By the time he graduated from high school, he had taught himself the skills to create Dean's first web site. Ironically, this computer technology amazed the man who would argue throughout his campaign that we were a nation desperately in need of technology to stay ahead. Garrett continued to update the site during his freshman year in college. At home, to maintain the discretion we both needed to do our jobs, we simply agreed not to discuss our work. It was a covenant neither of us ever broke.

Now my bosses at the AP suggested that I ask Garrett not to take a job in the Dean campaign. However, I said that he was an adult and I would not stand in his way. The AP decided that I had a conflict of interest and ordered me to neither write nor edit any stories about the campaign. My decision was both painful and ironic. I never had second thoughts about the correctness of my choice, but it meant that after spending almost twelve years covering a politician, and becoming, in the process, one of the nation's most experienced analysts of Dean's behavior and policies, I would not be able to cover a presidential campaign that was accelerating and taking exciting, surprising turns.

I stayed engaged with the campaign in other ways, however. I spent most of the summer and fall fielding questions about Dean's record in

Vermont from AP reporters, as well as reporters and editors from other news organizations. And I watched, as did the rest of the nation, as Dean fever spread, culminating in August when Dean appeared on the covers of both *Time* and *Newsweek* in the same week. He launched the "Sleepless Summer Tour" and attracted 5,000 people in Portland, 10,000 in Seattle and another 10,000 in New York City. I watched with fascination as the campaign used the Internet to raise record amounts of money—whenever it deemed necessary—thanks to the symbolic gimmick of the baseball bat.

This was a frustrating time for me as the other presidential campaigns twisted parts of Dean's record in Vermont and then leaked the information to national political reporters, too many of whom accepted the distortions as truth. Fortunately, others called us to help them separate the truth from the distortions. Those members of the national press consumed by the "Gotcha!" mentality surprised me because they were so caught up in the frenzy of the moment that they were willing to report critical leaks from Dean's opponents, without regard for the bias of the sources, simply in order to beat their competition into print. One story, in particular, caught us off guard. Dick Gephardt attacked Dean for giving tax breaks to Enron, claiming "the governor was engaging in gross hypocrisy," because Dean was, at the same time, criticizing President Bush for giving tax breaks to indicted businessmen Dean referred to as "Ken Lay and the boys." Several news organizations jumped on the story and repeated it the following week when Gephardt stepped up the attacks and accused Dean of giving "windfalls" to "corporate criminals.... While he was attacking President Bush's special treatment of Enron, he's been hiding the fact that he turned Vermont into a tax shelter for that very same corporate criminal."

No one in Vermont—no reporter or state official or business person or politician—could understand Gephardt's charge, which John Kerry nonetheless then picked up. At issue was the state's captive insurance industry, which had been started by Republican Gov. Richard

Snelling, in 1981, and which had continued and grown under every governor since, Republican and Democrat. Captive insurance companies are a mechanism allowing corporations to self-insure while they still receive tax deductions for the premiums they pay. Before Vermont started to pursue the market, most corporations had set up their captives in Bermuda or the Cayman Islands. Vermont's aggressive courting of the captives brought that business back to the states and generated millions of dollars for Vermont. In 1993 Dean had signed a law that cut state taxes on the premiums paid to the captives, part of an effort to entice more business to the state. It worked, with the number of captives more than doubling from 257 in 1992 to 597 at the end of 2002. Enron was one of the corporations to set up its captive insurance program in Vermont after the tax cut became law. It is a complicated story, but both Gephardt and Kerry played it for their own advancement. In fact, Vermont did not do anything special for Enron, but Dean was the subject of negative stories for more than a week for giving secret tax breaks to Ken Lay.

> **On the night of The Scream I was flying back to Vermont from a vacation with my wife and daughter, Lindsay, and watched in disbelief in an airport lounge as CNN showed Dean in third place, behind John Kerry and John Edwards.**

On the night of The Scream I was flying back to Vermont from a vacation with my wife and daughter, Lindsay, and watched in disbelief in an airport lounge as CNN showed Dean in third place, behind John Kerry and John Edwards. The analysts had been saying Iowa was a fight for first between Dean and Dick Gephardt, who came in fourth. We would later learn how Kerry, discarded by the media, had quietly organized the state, capitalizing on the mechanisms of a caucus vote, and how Iowa voters tired of the mudslinging between Gephardt and Dean were opting for the more positive candidacies of Kerry and Edwards. Although much attention focused on The Scream, which was played and replayed hundreds and hundreds of times, I think the campaign was over before Dean grabbed that microphone and pledged to go on to "South Carolina and Oklahoma and Arizona and North Dakota and New Mexico!" He had lost Iowa, and lost it badly. The irony, of course, is that back when he left the governor's office in 2003, he had not the slightest expectation of winning Iowa—or of even really being on the national radar in January of 2004. In his best case scenario, he would do well in the New Hampshire primary and maybe get enough of a bounce out of New Hampshire to be taken seriously. But along came the war in Iraq, and Dean's keen political sense exposed voters' frustrations with their leaders—and his call to take the country back resonated with many.

Dean returned to Burlington on February 18, 2004, a day after finishing third in Wisconsin, the state he said would be his last best hope to remain a contender. His speech that day in Burlington showed how far he had come and how much he had learned. His campaign's battle cry—"You have the power!"—thundered powerfully throughout the Sheraton Hotel's conference room. Now, he told the standing-room only crowd, it was time for everyone to understand that he meant it:

> And now that the campaign is stopped, I'm going to say something that all of you have heard me say before.
>
> But I want you to think about it now because now is the most important time that you have heard it. And this is the real message of this campaign and you'll hear it in a different way because I am no longer a candidate.
>
> The biggest lie that people like me tell people like you at election time is that, If you vote for me, I'll solve your problems. The truth is the power is in your hands, not mine.
>
> Abraham Lincoln said that a government of the people, by the people, and for the people shall not perish from this Earth. You have the power to take back the Democratic Party and make us stand up for what's right again.

Allow us to fulfill the dream of Harry Truman in 1948 that he laid out where we would no longer be the last industrial country on the face of the Earth without health insurance.

Allow us to stand up again for the rights to organize for ordinary men and women. Allow us to stand again for the principles of equal rights under the law for every single American.

You have the power to take our country back so that the flag of the United States of America no longer is the exclusive property of John Ashcroft and Dick Cheney and Rush Limbaugh and Jerry Falwell; that it belongs to all of us again.

And together we have the power to take back the White House in 2004, and that is exactly what we're going to do.

In June 2004, after the collapse of his campaign, Dean and I met for lunch at Pauline's Kitchen, in South Burlington. He was providing his first in-depth interview about his presidential campaign. Appearing relaxed, wearing a sweater and jeans, he talked for more than two hours. He said his campaign caught fire because "there was this enormous vacuum, and the Washington guys didn't get it until much later. People were ready for the message." As for the campaign's collapse, Dean quickly and almost dispassionately ticked off three reasons for its failure: Kerry did a great job organizing and winning the Iowa caucuses, his own campaign peaked too early, and his campaign never had the time to build the infrastructure needed to fuel the effort.

One of his most poignant memories was of a woman in a wheelchair who gave him $50 in quarters at a breakfast meeting in Iowa. The money came from her federal supplemental income check. "Even now I can hardly tell that story," Dean said, his voice breaking. "She said she had been saving the quarters for two years, when she could, for something that was really important — and this was really important to her." Dean said it was hard coming to grips with the sacrifices and trust of his legions of devoted supporters. "I am pretty overwhelmed.

I don't really feel I let them down, I must say, but I am pretty shocked not just by how supportive they were, but what they were willing to do."

It was those supporters—and perhaps a nagging concern about disappointing them—that kept Dean on the road six days a week, long after his personal campaign had ended. He campaigned for others with the same energy and zeal that marked his own pursuit of the presidency. Gone were the chartered planes and the entourage. No press planes. No aides. Just Howard Dean. "I think if I had dropped out of the race on February 18 and said that was that, that would have been a terrible thing to do," he said, his voice once again breaking. "Because it would have just been about me—and it never was."

Bernie Sanders won election to the U.S. House in 1990 as an independent.

"It's good for both parties to have a thorn in their side."

— *U.S. Rep. Leon Panetta, 1991*

Chapter 9

Bernie

Bernie Sanders jabs at the air, his flushed face a sharp contrast to his unruly white hair as he unleashes one of his patented attacks on Washington, the Congress and the president.

"The government that we have today in the White House, the House of Representatives with Tom Delay, the Senate with Bill Frist, is the most right-wing, extremist government, perhaps in the history of the United States," he bellows at labor activists attending a May Day celebration in Barre's century-old Labor Hall.

"Time after time they pass legislation that benefits the rich and the powerful, and they pass legislation that hurts the middle class, working people and low income people."

The crowd roars. They love it. This is Bernie at his best: one-part revivalist preacher, two parts theater, and an equal measure of passionate ideology, all served up with biting sarcasm. It is vintage Bernie. Literally. The words and message have not changed in more than thirty years. Tens of thousands of times in his still unmistakable Brooklyn accent he has decried as outrageous "the growing gap between the rich and the poor."

Standing in the back of the Labor Hall I marveled at how far Sanders had come and how little his message had changed. Sixteen years after being elected to the U.S. House, he could still bring crowds to their feet with his Congress-bashing. In the process, he had become such a fixture in Vermont's political landscape that he had virtually lost his last name. Everywhere he goes, he is simply "Bernie."

Now he seems headed to the U.S. Senate, the nation's most exclusive club. When he first ran for the U.S. Senate—in a special election in January 1972—he won a mere two percent of the vote. In 1974, the last time he ran for the Senate, he garnered all of four percent. Sanders also ran twice for governor in the 1970s, always running under the banner of the leftist Liberty Union. For his efforts, he won one percent and six percent, respectively. Vermonters largely considered him an entertaining political gadfly. He was praised for his passion and his theatrics but dismissed as a perennial candidate, a fringe candidate.

I first met Bernie in the fall of 1974 when he came to Middlebury College for a U.S. Senate debate. His hair was much darker but just as unruly; his criticism of politics and mainstream politicians just as pointed. In his remarks Sanders asked Pat Leahy, the Democratic nominee, if it was morally right that someone should have the wealth of a Rockefeller while people were going hungry. Leahy responded by detailing his proposals to close tax loopholes, but before he finished his thought, Sanders interrupted: "Pat didn't answer the question," he said. "The reason he didn't answer it is that he has to answer to the folks back in Winooski. They think that if Pat Leahy says it's morally wrong that some people have billions while other people have none—which Pat may, in fact, think—they're going to think he is a commie, and they're going to vote for Richard Mallary [the Republican]."

After his 1976 loss in the gubernatorial race Sanders left the Liberty Union and appeared to give up politics. He produced a documentary on his hero Eugene Debs. Debs, founder of the American Socialist Party and a six-time candidate for president, was a man whose political success and unwavering devotion to his ideas mirrored his own. For the time being, Sanders seemed content with a career producing educational materials.

In 1980, however, a friend showed Sanders that while he had won only six percent of the statewide tally in the 1976 gubernatorial race, he had doubled that percentage in Burlington; in some of the city's working-class wards he had attracted sixteen percent. His friend, Richard Sugarman, suggested that if Sanders concentrated all of his energy on his hometown he might be able to defeat the five-term incumbent mayor, Democrat Gordon Paquette, in the March 1981 election. Sanders ran and ousted Paquette, then 64 and a former baker, by ten votes. In retrospect it is easy to see how: Sanders, who was 39 at the time, campaigned hard, opposing Paquette's proposed increase in the property tax as well as a real estate developer's plan to construct condominiums on the city's waterfront. He picked up support from the Burlington Patrolman's Association, which was quite a coup, and assembled an extremely diverse coalition.

> The win may seem probable in hindsight, but no one saw it coming. My memory is that we didn't even have a reporter in Burlington that night, but we rushed one over following the announcement of his win.

The win may seem probable in hindsight, but no one saw it coming. My memory is that we didn't even have a reporter in Burlington that night, but we rushed one over following the announcement of his win. And although Sanders ran as an independent, the national news media, including the AP, played up the fact that he considered himself a socialist. Sanders' victory won worldwide play in the media: Cartoonist Garry Trudeau devoted a Sunday edition of his "Doonesbury" cartoon to Sanders; soon people were referring to the city as "The People's Republic of Burlington." Our phones rang incessantly, and we began then what continued through the years, that is, patiently explaining that yes, Sanders is a socialist but with a small "s." He considers himself a democratic-socialist and is not a member of the Socialist Party. Rarely did that distinction register, and to this day most references to Sanders call him a Socialist.

Following the flush of victory, though, came the reality of city politics. Sanders had dozens of ideas but only two supporters on the thirteen-member City Council. Those who didn't support him took the approach that they would merely wait out the mayor's two years in office and then work for his defeat. The establishment was scared to death by Sanders' win, and with good reason. The day after the election Sanders proclaimed, "The decisions in this city are not going to be made in the offices of banks and big businesses any more." The president of the local hospital said, "I almost drove off the road" when he heard on his car radio that Sanders had won.

The City Council rejected Sanders' nominees for top city posts, with one board member saying, "I cannot support your nominations because it is a method to expand the Socialist Party in the city of Burlington." Sanders pushed on, undeterred, using volunteers to help him build and promote his agenda designed to open up the waterfront and bring new people into the city and into city government.

A year later three of Sanders' supporters won seats on the Council, which then reluctantly began to accept the fact that his election was not a fluke. He won re-election bids in 1983, 1985 and 1987.

Sanders ventured back into state politics in 1986 with a run for governor. He was in his third term as mayor at the time, and he ran as an independent. Gov. Madeleine Kunin, a Democrat, was seeking her second term, and the Republican candidate was Lt. Gov. Peter Smith. Again, Sanders did not fare well in a statewide contest. Many Democrats were upset that he was challenging Kunin, who had a strong environmental record and who was also the state's first woman gover-nor. Not without reasons, liberals feared Sanders would split the vote and thereby promote a Republican to the state's top office. In the end, he won just fifteen percent of the vote.

In 1988, Sanders returned to statewide politics with a run for the U.S. House. This time his opponents were Smith and Democrat Paul Poirier. This was a fascinating campaign. To me it was more interesting than the one in 1990 that Sanders had actually won. This was the year when Vermonters began to look at Sanders as more than just a spoiler; this was a year when Vermonters, more than ever before, put personal-ity ahead of party, allowing him to beat the Democratic nominee.

This was also the year in which Sanders began to attack the AP for its coverage of his campaign, attacks that grew more strident and aggressive in 1990 and culminated with sharp and direct criticism of me in 1991.

But first the campaigns. In politics, where timing and momentum are everything, Sanders in 1988 had a summer and fall most politi-cians can only dream of. The only thing that didn't go his way was the final tally. The 1988 campaign showed how unpredictable politics really is, and how much campaigns owe to luck and a combination of intangi-bles. With no incumbent in the race the contest was wide open, and Sanders had the advantage of having run previous statewide campaigns. This gave him confidence, a good organization from his 1986 guberna-torial bid and standing among the electorate. Paul Poirer, in contrast, was making his first statewide run. Widely praised as a competent, successful Democratic leader in the state House, Poirier, of Barre, was unable to translate that reputation into statewide appeal. His campaign hit its high point the week after the primary and then plummeted.

Above all, though, Sanders gained from the strong, clear image he had instilled in the voters. His reputation as a fighter against the estab-lishment had been carefully crafted in his terms as mayor and his 1986 gubernatorial campaign; his platform of forcing the wealthy and corporations to pay higher taxes was ingrained in the minds of the electorate. And a race for the U.S. House seemed a good match for his iconoclasm. With Vermont having only a single representative in the 435-member House, Vermonters seemed receptive to the idea of electing a high-profile person who wouldn't be intimidated by the 434-to-1 odds. The final boost in 1988 was money. Unlike 1986, when money was a problem for Sanders, he had the cash in 1988, less than Smith but more than Poirier.

All of these elements mixed together in that mystical combination that gives campaigns momentum. At some point in the fall, but long before November, Sanders did what he had to do: He persuaded people he could win. That perception was critical if Sanders wanted a credible showing, and it was essential if he hoped to win, because in politics perception is reality, and for so many years Sanders had been viewed as the spoiler of statewide races.

As increasing numbers of Democrats abandoned Poirier for Sanders — with former Attorney General M. Jerome Diamond leading the charge — more Vermonters than ever before decided a Sanders win was possible.

The changing perception started with political insiders who began talking about the possibility of a Sanders win. Political reporters began speculating about it, and increasing numbers of ordinary Vermonters began discussing it. That changing perception gave the possibility legs. Following his defeat, Poirier said he believed the press at some point decided it wanted Sanders to win and tried to make that happen. But there was no collective decision. The press competes; it rarely holds hands. What happened was that the press reported on the changing perception among the political insiders and eventually among Vermonters, and that in itself contributed to an exponential spreading of the word. The press fueled the fire, but it did not start it.

The fire was real, though. It sent a panic through the Smith campaign because it seemed to be out of control. As increasing numbers of Democrats abandoned Poirier for Sanders—with former Attorney General M. Jerome Diamond leading the charge—more Vermonters than ever before decided a Sanders win was possible. In their minds, Poirier became the spoiler.

On election night the early returns put Sanders up by ten points. However, soon his lead dropped to five points, and then he and Smith stayed even for several hours. Smith eventually pulled ahead by three percentage points, and the final tally was Smith 41 percent, Sanders 38 percent and Poirier 19. That night, though, was not the loss it seemed for Sanders; it was a turning point.

That year Sanders and I disagreed often about the AP's coverage of his campaign. He thought we had ignored him in favor of Smith and Poirier. All candidates complain about how the press portrays them, and all candidates voice displeasure when their news conferences and position papers don't generate stories and headlines.

Sanders' criticism, however, was in a whole different league. Take the day in 1988 when he showed up at our office—then above the Thrush—with a camera crew from the CBS news program, *60 Minutes*, which was in the state to profile Vermont's most prominent radical. This is how Sanders describes that event in his 1997 book, *Outsider in the House*:

> While they [CBS] were here, I held a press conference about agricultural issues on a farm in central Vermont. The Associated Press, the most important print media organization in the state, did not show up—which was getting to be a habit with them.
>
> When you're a politician dealing with the media, life is difficult. If you're getting screwed by the media, you don't have much recourse. Who can you complain to? They own the camera. They print the news. What are you going to do about it?
>
> Finally, for the one and only time in my life, I did have a recourse.

I had *60 Minutes* following me around. I could expose the AP to the world. A politician's dream come true.

"Come on, guys," I told my staff. "We're going to visit the AP and talk about fair news coverage." Ten minutes later I was walking up the stairs of the AP office in Montpelier, the camera and the microphone of *60 Minutes* right behind me. This time I was asking the questions. "Okay, how come you never cover my press conferences? You have time for the Republicans. You have time for the Democrats. Why not an independent?" The AP had heard it all before. Except this time the cameras of *60 Minutes* were rolling, and AP was on the defensive. It was delicious.

I had a lot of fun that afternoon. Of course, I paid for it later. You never beat the media. After I was elected in 1990, the AP chief went to Washington to do a long series on whether or not I was an effective congressman. Guess what he concluded?

But that's all over now. It's water over the dam. It's hardly worth remembering. The AP and I are friends now, and we have a truly professional relationship. Right? Right? Hello. Hello.

I was at home eating lunch when Sanders and the *60 Minutes* team barged into our office. While someone on my staff listened to Sanders' rant, someone else stepped into a back room and called me. I live less than a mile from the Thrush, so I arrived within a few minutes, ran up the stairs and went into the offices through a back door. Reading Sanders' description of the moment—"AP was on the defensive. It was delicious"—is not the way I remember it. I did not feel defensive at all (although I was angry at Sanders' stunt). I informed him we did not cover his news conference because it simply was not newsworthy. My news policy was to avoid the made-for-TV news conferences in which politicians stand on farms and say we need to do more to save farmers. That isn't news; that is opportunism. Maybe someday we can get the tape from the CBS vault and see whose version is more accurate.

The 1990 rematch between Smith and Sanders was about as ugly as they come. As the years have passed and Sanders' political strength has grown, analysts have tended to look back at the 1990 campaign as one that was Sanders' to lose. It wasn't. Smith, the incumbent, entered the race as the frontrunner, and the Sanders' campaign seemed in disarray through much of the summer and into the fall. After taking office in 1989, Smith had worked hard to exploit the power of incumbency and to position himself as a congressman who could make things happen even as a freshman. In late July Sanders stumbled into a weeks-long controversy over how he paid his staff—as consultants rather than employees—an arrangement that meant he did not have to pay the employer's share of the Social Security tax or unemployment insurance. The state Republican Party had called attention to the matter, describing it as a way for Sanders to avoid taxes, which the GOP said was hypocritical of a candidate complaining about the wealthy not paying its fair share of taxes.

Sanders responded, as he often does, by blaming the news media. He singled out one of my reporters, Sue Allen, for unfairly blowing the issue out of proportion. He also stated categorically that the "manner in which the Sanders for Congress campaign staff pays its campaign workers is totally proper, totally legal, and is the way our campaign workers have chosen to be paid." Unfortunately for Sanders, that turned out not to be so. In late August, the state Department of Employment and Training ruled that Sanders' campaign workers were, in fact, employees and the campaign had to pay unemployment taxes.

Polling in late September showed Smith and Sanders even with roughly a fifth of the voters undecided. But then the world fell apart for Smith. It began with his early support for a complex budget compromise worked out between the Congress and Bush White House that called for tax increases—including an increase in the gasoline tax—combined with spending cuts, including cuts in Medicare appropriations that would be offset by increased premiums and deductibles for seniors. Smith said the alternative was economic chaos and recession; Sanders called the deal horrendous, a slap in the face for seniors and the middle class. Within a week, opposition to the budget package had spread across the country. When it came up for vote on October 4, it was defeated 179-204. Smith voted for it, but most Republicans did not. The impasse kept Congress in session, which meant Smith could not return to the state to campaign at a critical moment.

Polling in mid-October showed Sanders gaining strength, particularly among senior citizens. He hammered away at the budget deal, saying it showed how out of touch the Congress was with the needs of ordinary people. His speeches echoed the themes of his Liberty Union races in the 1970s and laid the foundation for what would be the theme of his 2006 race for the U.S. Senate. "To me, the major issue of this campaign is a very simple one: Do you believe that the United States Congress today represents the needs of ordinary Americans, of working people, of the elderly? Or is it, in fact, a Congress significantly bought and sold by large corporations and wealthy individuals who are using that Congress for their own personal gain?"

Smith, on the defensive over the budget deal, then made the first of two dramatic moves to regain traction in the campaign. Both failed miserably. On Tuesday, October 23, President George H. W. Bush flew into Burlington to raise money for Smith. At a GOP breakfast, as the president and the White House press corps looked on, Smith criticized some of Bush's stands, saying at one point, "My specific disagreements with this administration are a matter of record." Smith spoke honestly and hoped to improve his image as an independent, but the remarks were reported as a sharp slap to the president.

A week later Smith took to the airwaves with a television ad attacking Sanders as a socialist who had said he was physically nauseated by John F. Kennedy's inaugural, who had praised Fidel Castro's Cuba and who had called the Democratic Party "ideologically bankrupt." The ad ended bitterly: "These are not Vermont values, Bernie.

Keep Vermont proud. Keep Peter Smith in Congress." The Smith campaign called the ad "powerful, honest and factual," but Sanders termed it "vicious, dishonest Red-baiting." Unfortunately for Smith, many voters sided with Sanders. Newspapers, even *The Burlington Free Press*, which had endorsed Smith, called on him to pull the ad. The *Barre-Montpelier Times Argus* published an editorial claiming that many of Smith's hometown neighbors "are genuinely sad to see what politics has done to a decent man." On election night it wasn't even close. Sanders won by sixteen points.

Sanders' relationship with the AP deteriorated during the 1990 campaign, which wasn't easy considering how bad things were in 1988. According to Steven Rosenfeld, Sanders' press secretary in the 1990 campaign, Sanders considered the AP to be "pro-Smith." Sanders was especially upset by coverage of the debate over whether his campaign workers were, in fact, employees rather than self-employed consultants. Rosenfeld, in his book on the campaign, *Making History in Vermont*, recounts numerous conversations about the employee-consultant dispute in which Sanders described the AP as biased against him. "They're really on the take," he said at one point in a conversation in his office. Sue Allen wrote the series of stories on this issue for the AP, and time proved her stories to be accurate. But Sanders used this issue and Sue's stories to unleash another unpleasant attack on the AP. At a news conference on the State House lawn on July 27, Sanders argued once more that his treatment of his staff as consultants was legal. He then criticized the AP for focusing on this story rather than on his stands on the issues.

"We have sent out press releases to The Associated Press on important issues that were not picked up," Sanders charged. Then he changed

> "To me," said Sanders, "the major issue of this campaign is a very simple one: Do you believe that the United States Congress today represents the needs of ordinary Americans, of working people, of the elderly?"

his voice to mock what he thought the AP response would be. "That's kind of boring, Bernie; that's just healthcare issues." Continuing, he mocked what he thought our response would be to the employee press release: "This is good juicy stuff. We can run this on the front pages for weeks."

When the questioning at the news conference finally began, Anson Tebbetts, then with WDEV radio and now with WCAX-TV, asked, "Are you saying The Associated Press is biased?"

"Yes, I do believe so," said Sanders. He then tried to change the subject, but the other reporters began sharply questioning him on his opinion. At one point he started to walk away, but the reporters kept pelting him with questions on the subject. Again he leveled his charge: "Do I think that The Associated Press is pro-Smith? Yeah, I do," but he refused to elaborate or give examples. Instead, he said he would discuss it at another time.

I did not attend the news conference, but I heard about it from Sue Allen as soon as she returned to the office. I listened to the tape in disbelief. Sanders' dissatisfaction with our coverage did not surprise me, but the timing did. Just two days before, he and I had discussed his complaints in detail, a discussion that I thought allowed him to air his grievances and allowed me to explain why we had done what we had done. We had ended the conversation on a positive note, with me asking him to call me directly at the office or at home anytime he had a specific complaint. What further surprised me was the way he had blurted out his complaints with us at a State House news conference called on an entirely different subject, impetuous criticism that distracted from his main message and put him on record as saying in a very public session that he felt the AP was biased. His doing so, in effect, put a ball and chain around his ankle. Throughout the rest of the campaign, try as he might to stay on message with his platform, the topic of his relations with the AP inevitably raised its head over and over again.

Sanders was not the first candidate to complain about the AP's coverage of his campaign. In my 25 years running the Vermont bureau I can't think of a candidate or governor who did not complain at one time or another about our political coverage. In the 1980s I had purposely moved us away from covering candidate news conferences, feeling that they were merely attempts by the campaigns to manage the news and to set the agenda according to their terms. Sanders' outrage over the failure of the Congress to raise the minimum wage was not news. I felt our time was better spent doing a mixture of candidate profiles, on-the-campaign trail stories and issue stories. In 1988, for example, I assigned our reporters the task of writing profiles of the candidates without once mentioning anything about their political lives, assignments that produced a series of excellent and revealing biographies.

With Sanders' victory came lots of national press attention but also some thorny questions as the leadership in the House tried to figure out what to do with him. It had been nearly half a century since the election of a true independent who did not affiliate with the Democratic or Republican parties after the election. At first the Democrats, upset with his harsh criticism of the party during the campaign, didn't want anything to do with Sanders. He was the odd man out: an independent in an institution that revolves around the two-party system; a socialist in a chamber dominated by moderates and conservatives; a freshman in a world that favors seniority. As abrasive as ever, his style clashed rudely in an institution that rewards collegiality.

Six months into his first term, I went down and spent a week in Washington to get a sense of how he was faring. In his 1997 book Sanders claimed this was payback for his 1988 ambush of our office with the *60 Minutes* crew. It wasn't. I simply was curious how the first independent member of Congress in forty years was faring. I filled plenty of notebooks with criticism from members of Congress who were tired of Sanders' unrelenting attacks on them and on the institution. Rep. Barney Frank, a liberal Democrat, denounced Sanders as completely ineffective "because he offends just about everyone. His holier-than-thou attitude—saying in a very loud voice he is smarter than everyone else and purer than everyone else—really undercuts his effectiveness. To him, anybody who disagrees with him is a crook." Even Senators Jim Jeffords and Pat Leahy admitted to being upset with Sanders. Jeffords was the more outspoken, saying, "Obviously, I disagree with his style and I think he is counterproductive."

However, Sanders had his supporters, too. Rep. Joseph Kennedy, D-Mass, said "this place needs to be shaken up," and Leon Panetta said of Sanders, "It's kind of refreshing to the institution; it's good for both parties to have a thorn in their side."

> I followed Sanders for several days, watching him work in committee, and we sat down for a series of lengthy interviews. Sanders made no attempt to hide his disgust at the ways of Washington.

I followed Sanders for several days, watching him work in committee, and we sat down for a series of lengthy interviews. Sanders made no attempt to hide his disgust at the ways of Washington. "This place is not working," he told me. "Change is not going to take place until many hundreds of people are thrown out of their offices." My series of articles generally portrayed Sanders as an outsider in the House, which ironically, considering his complaints about my articles, was the title of his own book about being in Congress. After the series ran in newspapers, Sanders said I had "overstepped the bounds of responsible journalism" and that the articles were the result of "a reporter's personal vendetta." In letters to newspapers around the state and to AP management, he argued that I had spoken only with mainstream members of Congress, "people I have been fighting for twenty years. Ask Pepsi what they think about Coke and you might get a similar response."

I think Sanders overreacted to my stories but I can see why he did. What I wrote was accurate: He had campaigned as an outsider, he held the Congress and many of its members in low regard and he found the ways of Washington far more frustrating than he had ever imagined. The overall perception given by my stories, though, was that his strong opinions made it difficult for him to be effective in that body—and that's not an impression you want to give to voters.

Much changed in the next fifteen years as Sanders adapted to the ways of Washington. Over the years the Democrats who denounced him accepted him. Republicans who ridiculed his socialist philosophy ended up signing on as occasional co-sponsors of his legislative initiatives. Most importantly, Sanders realized the importance of coalitions—and he began to forge them. He formed the Progressive Coalition, with more than fifty members, which gave him an important bloc of votes and some negotiating power. He reached out to Republicans, pulling together disparate groups of people when interests merged.

"Do I work better with people than I used to? Yeah, I do," said Sanders when I interviewed him in 2005. "That's simply a learning curve, knowing how to reach out, how to put together coalitions, getting to know people in a way perhaps that I now do better than I did before."

For many of his years in the House, Sanders has continued to voice frustration with the coverage of the AP, and I think some of his complaints have had merit. The AP and other news organizations in Vermont do an incomplete job of covering the congressional delegation. The Washington bureau of the AP covers Congress as an institution, but the Vermont bureau under my tenure never had the resources to adequately follow what the two senators and one member of the House were doing. We reported on key votes, but it was impossible for us to follow all that was going on. Several times, though, I went to Washington to report on the delegation and to see how Sanders was adapting to the ways of the Hill.

In 1999 I sat in on a meeting of the House Banking Committee as Sanders, a committee member, offered an amendment to HR21, a bill to create a disaster reinsurance fund that, in essence, would lessen the risks for insurance companies when catastrophes strike. "Mr. Chairman," he said, "this amendment is simple and straightforward. All it does is replace the entire text of the bill." Laughter rippled through the cavernous Wright Patman Room, and then Sanders launched a frontal attack on the bill, claiming it "represents an unnecessary taxpayer bailout for the insurance industry and is a rip-off to the American consumer." The language is vintage Sanders, yet there was a difference. Sanders had two Republicans and one Democrat joining him as cosponsors. He had lined up support from a wide variety of groups, including the U.S. Business and Industry Council, the National Taxpayers Union and Citizens Against Government Waste. The Republican chairman of the committee called the amendment the most important of the eighteen before the panel. In the end Sanders lost 23-31, but watching him in action that day made it clear that he was no longer the outsider in the House.

> "If you ask me what my dream is as a political person, it is to allow this state to do what no other state in the union has done: to stand up to the establishment, the big-monied people, to the Democrats and Republicans and show the rest of the country that it can be done."
> — Bernie Sanders

Back in 1986, as Sanders campaigned for governor, he sat down with one of my reporters, John Donnelly, in a Barre restaurant. He talked about growing up in his working-class family in Brooklyn and constant fights about money. "Money was an issue of pre-eminent importance in my family," he said. "It caused a lot of bickering between my mother and my father." Then he talked about his reasons for getting into politics. "If you ask me what my dream is as a political person, it is to allow this state to do what no other state in the union has done: to stand up to the establishment, the big-monied people, to the Democrats and Republicans and show the rest of the country that it can be done.

"If that happens, my life's work will have been successful."

Sen. Patrick Leahy questions a witness before the Judiciary Committee.

"Mr. Leahy?" "No," said the senior senator from Vermont. "Mr. Leahy votes 'No,'" echoed the clerk.

Chapter 10

From "Landslide Leahy" to "Senator's Senator"

On February 28, 2006, the U.S. Senate was in the middle of debate on S.2271, a bill reauthorizing sections of the USA Patriot Act. One senator moved to cut off discussion, and the clerk started calling the roll.

"Mr. Akaka?" "No." "Mr. Akaka votes 'No,'" intoned the clerk.

"Mr. Alexander?" "Yes." "Mr. Alexander votes 'Yea.'"

The chant and refrain continued in the centuries-old tradition of a Senate roll call as senators rushed into the chamber in time to cast their votes with the clerk.

"Mr. Leahy?" "No," said the senior senator from Vermont. "Mr. Leahy votes 'No,'" echoed the clerk.

Sen. Norm Coleman, of Minnesota, presiding over the chamber, announced the results of the vote: "On this vote the yeas are 69, the nays are 30. Three-fifths of the senators duly chosen and sworn having voted in the affirmative, the motion is agreed to."

Coleman then glanced down at the Democratic leader, Sen. Harry Reid, waiting to be recognized at the minority leader's desk. "Mr. President," began Reid, "today Pat Leahy, senior senator from Vermont, reached a Senate milestone, to say the least. A few minutes ago he cast his 12,000th vote. He has voted in the Senate 12,000 times. This is quite an accomplishment. He joins a very elite club."

Reid went on to praise Leahy as a "Senator's Senator. He is able to be as partisan as any senator we have, but he is also a person who can be as bipartisan as any senator who has ever served in the Senate." A parade of the leaders of the nation's most exclusive club took turns paying tribute to Leahy. Arlen Specter, the Pennsylvania Republican who chairs the Senate Judiciary Committee, said he and Leahy have worked together across the political aisle for more than 25 years. "It has been a very close working relationship, and never as close as it has been for the past fourteen months as we have worked together on the Judiciary Committee with some very significant accomplishments for the Senate and the American people." The Republican leader of the Senate, Bill Frist, talked about traveling all over the world into small villages and finding people who didn't know the majority leader, "but Pat Leahy's name comes up again and again from the underserved, from the people who have suffered the tragedy of landmine injuries. It is remarkable. . . to have real people thousands of miles away coming forward with his name. It reflects the great legacy he leaves [and] that he continues to leave."

"I must say that I was awed and humbled the first day I walked on the floor as a 34-year-old to be sworn in, where thirty minutes before I was the state's attorney sitting in a county in Vermont and thirty minutes later was then the junior senator from Vermont," Leahy said in his response to all this praise. "I still feel that same awe every time I walk on this floor. The day I stop feeling that awe, I will stop walking here. With that, I have said more than Vermonters usually do. I yield the floor."

Pat Leahy has come a long way. He is now considered unbeatable in Vermont. In 2004 he won a fifth term in the Senate with 71 percent of the vote; six years earlier he had received 72 percent. On December 27, 2008, before he finishes his current term, he will become the longest-serving senator in the history of Vermont, eclipsing the record set by his predecessor, George Aiken, of 33 years and 357 days. In the Senate—where seniority rules—only six of the body's 100 senators have more seniority than he does. Among the Democrats, only four do. He is the ranking Democratic member on the Judiciary Committee, the third-ranking Democrat on Appropriations and the second-ranking on Agriculture. Over the years he has chaired the Judiciary and Agriculture Committees, and depending on the ability of the Democrats to regain the majority, Leahy could very well end up chairing the most powerful committee in the Senate: Appropriations.

> **Pat Leahy has come a long way. He is now considered unbeatable in Vermont. In 2004 he won a fifth term in the Senate with 71 percent of the vote; six years earlier he had received 72 percent.**

These are astonishing achievements for someone who surprised everyone by winning election in 1974, and who barely held on to his seat six years later in the Republican landslide of 1980.

Leahy is a Montpelier native whose grandparents, Irish and Italian immigrants, worked the Barre quarries until they died, one from silicosis, the often-fatal lung disease associated with quarry dust. His father ran a printing firm, and Leahy delivered printing jobs throughout the city, errands that took him into the State House when he was young. In 1966, when Leahy was just 26, Gov. Phil Hoff appointed him Chittenden County state's attorney to finish someone else's term. Until then, the position had been regarded as part time. But Leahy made it full time, assuming the prosecution of all murder cases and significant felony cases, cases that previously had been handled by the attorney general's office or special prosecutors. Reflecting his skill or the amount of time he was now devoting to Chittenden County cases, or both, he won 32 guilty verdicts in his first 35 trials. His handling of his job gave him a high profile in the state's largest county, a profile he cultivated with many news conferences and television appearances.

Like many Vermonters in the 1970s I first encountered Leahy through skinny dipping. Leahy, then the state's attorney for Chittenden County, confronted one of the pressing issues of the day in law enforcement: Should skinny dippers be prosecuted? This was truly a hot-button issue in Vermont at the time. A judge in Washington County had sentenced a Warren man to twenty days in jail for skinny-dipping in the Mad River, but the state's attorney had dismissed the sentence and dropped the charge, opening up a fray between two branches of the law. Although Leahy had no standing in the case, his response to this little bit of theater attracted national attention in publications such as *Time*. He argued that nude bathing was unacceptable in public and semi-public areas, but a time-honored tradition on private land out of public view: "the State has no legitimate interest and swimmers should be left alone. . . in secluded areas sometimes publicly used (e.g., rivers, swimming holes, etc.): If no member of the public present is offended, no disorderly conduct has taken place." In Leahy's legal "opinion," if members of the public, such as families wishing to swim, complained, then the police officer should order the nude bather to dress. Summons to court would be issued only if the nude swimmers failed to stay clothed after being told to get dressed.

What earned Leahy's legal "opinion" such wide attention was his accompanying explanation of how he had arrived at his decision:

> I began by reviewing the Norman Rockwell paintings, thoughtfully resurrected by the American Civil Liberties Union, showing such activities taking place allegedly in Vermont (along this line I was unable to either confirm or refute the persistent rumor that Vermont's number one politician, Calvin Coolidge, had also engaged in such activity within the borders of this State while subject to Vermont laws). I have also

discussed—after grants of immunity—experiences of this nature enjoyed by some of Vermont's prosecutors, judges, law enforcement officers and sailboat operators. After checking the statute of limitations, I have even reviewed past histories with some of my contemporaries during my teenage years in Montpelier. Also, each member of my office offered to investigate this manner in an undercover manner (so to speak). It appears that most Vermonters I've talked to have engaged in such scandalous activity at some point in their life (with the exception of a couple I didn't believe who claimed to have done so in May. Everyone knows the high probability of frostbite in May in Vermont).

Such a clever elucidation showed Leahy's media savvy even back in his days as a prosecutor. Here was a guy who could turn almost anything into a media event. No wonder he was a darling of reporters who was able to attract publicity in a position that generally shuns it.

Early in 1974 Leahy announced that he would run for the U.S. Senate seat held by Sen. George Aiken, R-Vt. Then 81, Aiken had not yet revealed whether he would seek re-election, and many Vermonters criticized this upstart for daring to challenge the state's iconic senior senator. Some press accounts dismissed Leahy, born in 1940, the same year Aiken was first elected to the Senate, as too young and inexperienced. Furthermore, jumping from county prosecutor to the U.S. Senate was regarded as an overly ambitious leap. After all, Aiken had served as speaker of the House, lieutenant governor and governor before running for the U.S. Senate. The state's other senator, Bob Stafford, had served as attorney general, lieutenant governor, governor and a member of the U.S. House before moving up to the Senate. That's the way it was done.

On Valentine's Day Aiken made Leahy's quixotic quest a little easier by announcing that he would retire at the end of his term. Aiken's decision generated national attention, but he dismissed it in typical fashion by quipping, "The news media were a little short of material that day, so my announcement came in handy."

Within a week U.S. Rep. Dick Mallary, R-Vt., said he would seek Aiken's seat. Mallary had been the speaker of the House in 1967, when I first visited the State House as an eighth grader. He had won election to the Vermont House in 1960, representing the town of Fairlee and assuming the seat his mother had held in the 1950s before she won election to the state Senate. In the House he banded together with several other ambitious freshmen—newcomers such as Democrat Phil Hoff and Republican Franklin Billings—to push progressive legislation.

In addition, Leahy used television in new ways for Vermont. He aired a thirty-minute documentary about his life, something that seems pretty banal today, but in 1974 it was revolutionary.

The group called itself the Young Turks, and by 1963 Hoff was governor, Billings was speaker and Mallary was chairman of the House Appropriations Committee. Billings was still speaker in 1965 and oversaw the contentious session when reapportionment was enacted. Mallary followed in his footsteps the next year, when a host of progressive initiatives passed. A year after my first visit to the State House, the voters of Orange County elected Mallary a state senator; in 1971 he served as secretary of administration under Gov. Deane Davis, and then in 1972 he easily won election to the U.S. House.

In the old Vermont, Mallary would have been the perfect candidate for the U.S. Senate. Conservative but with a liberal streak—like a head of black hair shot through with white—he was a modest and soft-spoken former dairy farmer and a member of a well-known and respected family. Moreover, he was a Republican in a state that had never elected a Democrat to the U.S. Senate. By 1974, however, Leahy understood perfectly that Vermont's political environment was opening doors that had never been opened before. He campaigned as an activist, a consumer advocate and an environmentalist, challenging his opponent on practically every vote Mallary had cast in his short time in the

U.S. House. In addition, Leahy used television in new ways for Vermont. He aired a thirty-minute documentary about his life, something that seems pretty banal today, but in 1974 it was revolutionary. His wife, Marcelle, a member of the extended and well-connected Burlington Pomerleau family, was almost a secret weapon. She campaigned in northern Vermont, using her fluent French to court the French Canadians who populated many of those towns.

A week before the election, a poll conducted by Vincent Naramore, a St. Michael's College professor, showed Leahy down by thirteen points. Leahy called the poll "bogus." Later in the week Naramore released another poll, this one conducted solely in Chittenden County, the state's most Democratic county. According to its findings, Leahy and Frank Cain, the Democratic nominee for the U.S. House, were leading in Chittenden County, but Naramore predicted the margin was not enough to offset the expected Republican votes elsewhere in the state. On the Friday before the election the *Rutland Herald* ran a big front-page headline about the poll declaring, "Chittenden Poll Dooms Leahy, Cain." Leahy was more upset by the headline than the poll, denouncing the newspaper for overplaying the poll's significance and complaining that such a doomsday headline could become self-fulfilling in the election. Ironically, the *Rutland Herald* had earlier endorsed Leahy, saying, "This seems to be the year when a change might be good for Vermont, a year when the Watergate party should be expected to suffer some consequences at the polls for the malfeasance of the Nixon administration."

Election night was long. I was with Leahy at the Ramada Inn, in South Burlington. The race was in doubt until after midnight, when results finally came in from Colchester and cemented his victory. In the end Leahy received 70,629 votes; Mallary won 66,223; and Bernie Sanders, on the Liberty Union ticket, received 5,901.

Watergate was a huge handicap for Mallary, as it was for Republicans across the country. Nationally, the Democrats picked up four seats in the Senate and 49 seats in the House, pushing their majority in the House above the two-thirds mark. Joining Leahy in the Senate in 1975 as so-called Watergate babies were such Democrats as Gary Hart, of Colorado; Dale Bumpers, of Arkansas; and John Glenn, of Ohio.

Once in Washington, Leahy moved aggressively to show Vermonters he was working hard for their interests. He became the first senator in the country to install a toll-free "800" telephone number so that his constituents could contact him without charge. He often tells the story of being asked by Senate leaders to name the three committees on which he most wanted to serve, and of being warned that he would only be assured of getting assigned to one of them. His response to them was, "The Agriculture Committee, the Agriculture Committee, and the Agriculture Committee," a reply that warmed the hearts of Vermonters. Leahy also landed a coveted seat on the Senate Appropriations Committee, a key position in controlling the nation's purse and a position Leahy would use increasingly to Vermont's benefit as he climbed in seniority.

As the 1980 campaign season neared, the biggest question in Vermont politics was whether Republican U.S. Rep. Jim Jeffords would challenge Leahy. Jeffords had been elected to the House the same year Leahy went to the Senate, despite the general backlash caused by Watergate, and was completing his third term. Jeffords left no doubt he would relish the opportunity. "My primary criticism is that he wants too much to be a senator," said Jeffords of Leahy. "His security in office is so important to him that it upstages his desire to serve the people of Vermont. He has the image of being a conservative to conservatives, a moderate with moderates and a liberal with the liberals." Jeffords made disparaging references to Leahy's tendency in conversation to drop names of important people he had met or talked to recently. The Republican took polls, explored finances and strategy, but eventually decided the race was too risky. He opted, instead, to stay in the House.

Six other Republicans, however, were eager to challenge Leahy. They lined up in a hotly contested primary election that included record campaign spending by Jim Mullin, an unknown insurance agent from Williston, who spent $543,400 in the primary. He lost, nevertheless, to Stewart Ledbetter, a former banking and insurance commissioner, who made his mark with voters before the primary by taking a much-publicized 450-mile walk around the state visiting with Vermonters. I shared the roads with him for a while to get a taste of this novel campaign strategy, but I didn't stay with it long enough to wear out my shoes the way Ledbetter did.

The fall campaign was unpleasant for Leahy. I remember traveling with him on the campaign trail in late October, and being surprised at how exhausted and pale he looked. Ledbetter attacked Leahy hard on defense issues and the economy, but he had his own secret weapon: his Republican ally, Jim Jeffords, who had hit the campaign trail on his behalf. According to Jeffords, Leahy was guilty of political duplicity, namely, saying one thing in Vermont and then another in Washington. Leahy countered by making his Vermont heritage the centerpiece of his campaign theme: "Of Vermont; For Vermont." At nearly every campaign stop, he managed to tell voters he was a native while Ledbetter was a flatlander, born in New York.

Once again the Senate election was a cliffhanger. Leahy eked out a win with 49.8 percent of the vote compared to Ledbetter's 48.6, earning him the sobriquet in Washington of "Landslide Leahy," because he had yet to win a Senate election with more than fifty percent of the vote. Taken in a national context, though, Leahy was indeed lucky. While 1974 was kind to Democrats, 1980 was not, as Republicans rode Ronald Reagan's coattails. They picked up twelve seats in the Senate, the largest swing since 1958, and gained control of the Senate, 53-46. Among Leahy's highly regarded Democratic colleagues who fell to defeat were Frank Church, of Idaho; Birch Bayh, of Indiana; John Culver, of Iowa; and George McGovern, of South Dakota.

Leahy returned to Washington dispirited. He could not comprehend how he could have worked so hard for six years in the Senate and then come so close to defeat. The close vote cut especially deeply because Ledbetter was new to statewide politics. "Here I had worked harder than I ever had in my life," he said in a 1986 interview with the AP. "I thought, is it really worth it for all I gave up in my family, to spend all this time, when you can have someone come up here, hand him a script and go with it?"

> **Leahy's reaction to Snelling's announcement provided a glimpse of the campaign strategy he would employ against one of Vermont's most formidable Republicans: Ignore him.**

Unfortunately for Leahy, the election six years later wasn't any easier. In fact, it required more of him, both personally and strategically. On October 17, 1985, former Gov. Richard Snelling, bowing to intense pressure from the Reagan White House, entered the race. "My decision may surprise some," said Snelling in his announcement. "Frankly, it surprised me somewhat. One or two months ago, my answer would have been 'No'." Snelling called the Senate "a cozy group where nice men and women talk about the problem and do nothing at all."

However, Leahy's reaction to Snelling's announcement provided a glimpse of the campaign strategy he would employ against one of Vermont's most formidable Republicans: Ignore him. In my story that day I wrote, "Leahy was on the Senate floor Thursday and could not be reached for comment, his aides said. However, spokesman Joseph Jamale said Leahy probably would not comment, because that would only inflate the importance of Snelling's announcement." And that remained the campaign's line right up to the election: Leahy was too busy doing the people's work to respond to whatever Dick Snelling said. It was a risky strategy that could have backfired, and almost did at the end of the campaign, when Leahy became the object of ridicule for refusing to sit on the same platform with Snelling at a forum in Burlington.

Leahy assembled the best campaign organization ever to work in Vermont. Among the staffers were Mary Beth Cahill, who would go on to manage John Kerry's presidential bid in 2004, and John Podesta, who would become Bill Clinton's chief of staff. He raised and spent a record amount of money, to that point, and built, under the direction of David Clavelle, an unparalleled field operation. By election day the campaign had identified approximately 70,000-80,000 supporters, and every one of them received two telephone calls on election day to ensure they made it to the polls.

Most importantly, though, the campaign was on the offensive from the beginning. It left nothing to chance. The campaign press relations, under Deborah Graham, mastered the art of pro-active political spin, ensuring that stories came out the way the campaign wanted. In my case, the Leahy campaign, fearing I might display a bias toward Snelling, worked behind the scenes to neutralize that possibility. Whenever I wrote an article—no matter how innocuous—someone from the campaign called sympathetic newspaper editors and complained about what I had written. The editors then called me to pass on the criticisms. A series of letters to the editors—all written by different people in different parts of Vermont—began appearing in newspapers around the state, critical of stories I had written about Snelling's decision to challenge Leahy. One from the October 28, 1985, *Rutland Herald* ran under the headline "Consider Them 'Puffs'":

> The recent articles by Chris Graff concerning Snelling's future political plans have been classic examples of "puff" pieces. They have been utterly lacking in substance while affording the readers a view through rose-colored glasses of Snelling, businessman and politician, dutifully answering his party's call. Unlike coverage by other reporters that clearly showed that they had done their job by interviewing people like William Gray, Patrick Garahan, and others who would have insight

into the story, Graff rarely quotes anyone and brings no new information to light. One expects that reporters meet at least minimal standards of objectivity and balance. Graff, however, does not. In his story of Oct. 11, Graff spends three paragraphs describing the former governor's efforts to balance the federal budget but fails to note that Proposition One had been little more than an utter failure in both public relations and substantive terms. Graff also fails to mention that Snelling is responsible for the largest deficit in the history of Vermont. It was clearly Snelling's failure to foresee the effects of Reagan's tax cuts that is the primary cause of Vermont's current fiscal problems. Regrettably, Graff's articles read more like the work of a Snelling press aide than an AP reporter.

The letters and editors' criticisms upset me. I took all such comments seriously, especially those from readers and editors. I never grew hardened to criticism, nor did I ever ignore it. I started every story I ever wrote with the goal of making it fair. Over my three decades in journalism, I'm sure there were stories I could have handled better, but I eventually adopted the attitude that if everyone was accusing me of bias, then I must be pointed pretty well down the middle. It helped me to sleep better at night. Only years after the 1986 election did I learn that those letters were part of a Leahy campaign tactic involving pre-emptive strikes.

In November Leahy's strategy of overwhelming force and efficiency finally brought him the kind of validation he sought. He beat Snelling by a two-to-one margin. But it was an expensive win. Leahy spent $1.3 million, or $10 per vote, while Snelling spent $1.2 million, or $17 per vote. The campaign's spending record lasted twenty years, until the 2006 U.S. Senate race between Bernie Sanders and Richard Tarrant.

Democrats did well nationally in the 1986 elections, gaining eight seats in the Senate, which gave them majority control and positioned Leahy as chairman of the Senate Agriculture Committee, a chairmanship he would hold until 1995. As chairman, Leahy worked closely with Indiana Republican Richard Lugar to pass numerous initiatives, including the 1994 Leahy-Lugar Act that closed down 1,100 USDA offices. These closings were part of a government streamlining leading to the 1996 Freedom to Farm Act, which included innovative conservation, rural development and nutrition programs. Most importantly for Vermont, Leahy's clout helped win passage of the Northeast Dairy Compact, considered a necessity for the survival of Vermont's dairy farms.

In July 1987 news broke that Leahy was responsible for the most serious leak from the Senate Intelligence Committee in its ten-year history. At issue was the panel's draft report on the Iran-Contra weapons deals, a draft the committee had decided not to release. On January 8, though, NBC news began a series of stories detailing what was in the report, including the committee's conclusion that President Reagan, contrary to his assertions, had, in fact, authorized the resumption of arms shipments to Iran in exchange for the release of all U.S. hostages held by that country. As a firestorm spread through Washington in response to the NBC report, Leahy called Sen. David Boren, the chairman of the committee, to confess that he was responsible for the leak and to offer to resign. Boren and the vice chairman, Sen. William Cohen, accepted Leahy's resignation, but Leahy's complicity and his resignation from the committee were kept secret from other members and the public.

When news of the January leak and Leahy's resignation at that time inevitably came out in July, Leahy tried to control the damage to his reputation by downplaying his role in the leak, the significance of the leak and any link between the leak and his resignation from the committee. At first, for example, in an interview with me he admitted only that he had shown the reporter "a couple of unclassified pages" to prove that the committee wasn't holding back the report for political reasons. "I just used this to make a point, and then went on to another matter in another part of the building and left something that had been sitting on my desk for a week at that point," he told me. But Leahy conceded later that he had allowed the reporter to take the report from the building for several hours without putting any restrictions on its use.

At the end of that week a chastened Leahy returned to Vermont to apologize. "I was incredibly careless, and I apologize for that," he said at a tense Burlington news conference in which reporters heatedly questioned his version of the events. "I have paid a high price," he said. "It is very embarrassing. It has been of concern to me and my family, and I am sorry for them. That is a price, and it bothers me very much. I am sorry for it because some of the people I work with might feel I let them down."

> In 1989 Leahy persuaded the Senate to establish a War Victims Fund — which the Senate formally designated in 1995 as the "Patrick Leahy War Victims Fund"— to provide medical and other assistance to innocent casualties of the world's conflicts.

It was during these years that Leahy began his passionate, decades-long campaign against landmines. Traveling through Central America, Leahy had met a young boy who had lost a leg stepping on a landmine near his home. That chance meeting led to Leahy's crusade. In 1989 Leahy persuaded the Senate to establish a War Victims Fund—which the Senate formally designated in 1995 as the "Patrick Leahy War Victims Fund"—to provide medical and other assistance to innocent casualties of the world's conflicts. The fund, which disbursed $60 million in sixteen countries in its first decade, has been used primarily to produce artificial limbs for victims of landmine explosions. Leahy worked for a moratorium on the export of landmines, and then launched a global campaign for an agreement to ban the production, transfer, use and stockpiling of anti-personnel mines and to remove existing minefields within a set period of time. The so-called Ottawa convention was signed in 1997 and became effective a year later.

In 1992 Jim Douglas stepped forward to challenge Leahy, leaving many of us to wonder if Douglas had lost his marbles. If Leahy could so humiliate Richard Snelling, one of the most popular former governors in the state, how did Douglas, who had been secretary of state since 1981, think he could do any better? Nevertheless, he did, closing the gap in percentage points to eleven. Douglas was able to put Leahy on the defensive in a way Snelling never could—by zeroing in on Leahy's financial dependence on political action committees. Douglas hammered home the criticism that Leahy had been bought by special interests whose interests might not coincide with Vermont's. "When all of his money comes from Disneyland, Hollywood and everywhere else except Vermont, whose interest does he really represent?" asked Douglas at one news conference. In a gesture meant to represent his own commitment to the state, he was accepting contributions only from Vermonters. Douglas also aired a series of humorous, biting television ads to get out his message and worm under Leahy's skin. By the end of the campaign, Leahy was concerned enough about the traction Douglas was getting that he decided to stop accepting money from PACs.

In 1998 Jack McMullen appeared on Vermont's political scene to challenge Leahy's re-election. McMullen had an amazing resumé as a consultant in financial analysis, as a teacher at Harvard Law School, as an investment banker, and as an engineer with the U.S. Atomic Energy Commission. He also had a slew of degrees from Columbia University, Harvard Law School and Harvard Business School. But he was a newcomer to Vermont who had only set up permanent residence in the state the previous year. That, coupled with McMullen's wealth and campaign spending, gave the Leahy camp all it needed to saddle him with the label of a carpetbagger who was coming to the state to buy a Senate seat.

I handed the Leahy campaign some ammunition against McMullen that May simply by reporting on an interview I had conducted with former U.S. Sen. Robert Stafford. I decided to stop in and visit Stafford in Rutland, because I kept running into things named for him. That winter we had had a devastating ice storm, prompting President Clinton to declare the state a disaster area under the Robert T. Stafford Disaster Relief and Emergency Assistance Act. Our son was in college, so I had been working through the paperwork of the national Stafford loan program. My brother works at the University of Vermont, next door to what was then the brand new $10 million Robert T. Stafford Hall. My idea was to write a column about Stafford and his ubiquitous mark, not just on the buildings and programs bearing his name, but on his greatest legacy: the environmental initiatives he championed to protect the air we breathe and the water we drink, as well as the Superfund he created to clean up lands that have been catastrophically contaminated by all manner of pollutants.

Stafford is the last of the old-time Vermont politicians who climbed the ladder of political offices in the expected way. He was Rutland city prosecutor; Rutland County state's attorney; deputy state attorney general; attorney general; lieutenant governor; governor; member of the U.S. House from 1961 to 1971 and member of the U.S. Senate from 1971 to 1989. His was a remarkable journey, during which he evolved from a conservative hawk politician to what he calls a Republican-moderate.

As we talked that Tuesday afternoon, I asked him whether he knew McMullen. He said he did not, and went on to say, "I am bothered by people from another state or another part of the country with large sums of personal money suddenly moving to Vermont and running for office here. There ought not to be any sense that Vermont is for sale. I want to be fair to Mulholland, or whatever his name is, but generally speaking, I think it is more appropriate for a candidate for a major office to spend some time in Vermont and understand the problems the state faces before suddenly deciding to be a candidate for our top offices."

I instinctively corrected Stafford when he mispronounced McMullen's name, and at that point had no thought of using the mispronunciation in my story because I didn't want to embarrass Stafford. After I corrected him, though, he continued on, explaining that "when you combine all the features—having a lot of money and suddenly coming to Vermont—I don't think it is good for Vermont for Mr. Mulholland to run until he has been here a while and learned what we are like." And this time when he pronounced Mulholland, he drew the name out to three long syllables—MUL-HOL-LAND—staring at me as he did so. This guy knew exactly what he was doing: He was sending the message that the senior Republican in the state, a man who had spent 28 years in the Congress, had no idea who this fellow was, McMullen, or Mulholland, or whatever his name is.

When I wrote my story—with the lede: "Vermont's senior Republican statesman, former U.S. Sen. Robert Stafford, says Jack McMullen hasn't lived in Vermont long enough to represent the state in the U.S. Senate."—you could almost hear the impact of Stafford's withering dismissal on the McMullen campaign. And throughout the rest of the campaign, reporters and others often referred to McMullen as "Mulholland or whatever his name is."

> "I am bothered by people from another state or another part of the country with large sums of personal money suddenly moving to Vermont and running for office here," said Sen. Robert Stafford.

Of course, McMullen didn't survive the primary election to face Leahy that November. Tunbridge farmer Fred Tuttle all but destroyed McMullen in a few minutes of questioning about things Vermont, questions McMullen painfully could not answer. After winning the primary, however, Tuttle made things easy for his opponent. He heartily endorsed Leahy, and the two of them held some congenial joint appearances in what was truly the most bizarre campaign Vermont has ever seen. McMullen may have made a comeback in 2004, this time winning the Republican nomination, but he was handily defeated in November by Leahy, who won 71 percent of the vote.

When Leahy went to the Senate in 1975, he was a young man suddenly thrust into the nation's most exclusive club. There was truth in Jim Jeffords' early criticisms of Leahy, who did tend to name drop, but many of us would have done the same after meeting national political luminaries such as Hubert Humphrey or Barry Goldwater or after getting summoned to the White House for meetings. He also tried hard to come across as conservative to conservatives, moderate to moderates and liberal to liberals. Some of this parsing of labels was politically astute. In Vermont of the 1970s, politicians had to be careful not to appear too liberal. Over the years, though, as Vermont's politics generally have shifted to the left, Leahy has evolved into one of the most liberal members of the Senate. He also has a reputation as a Democratic pit bull, willing to tear into Republicans when the need arises.

No moment better reflects this than his encounter in the summer of 2004 with Vice President Dick Cheney. The two were in the Senate chamber for the Senate's annual photo session. Leahy crossed the aisle and joked with Cheney about being in Republican territory. Cheney complained about comments Leahy had made the previous day critical of Iraq contracts that had been won by Halliburton, Cheney's former employer, without any competitive bidding. Leahy responded, and then Cheney, in the delicate explanation used by *The Washington Times*, "responded with a barnyard epithet, urging Mr. Leahy to perform an anatomical sexual impossibility." The press ate it up, and once again little Vermont looked to the nation like a model of courage and integrity.

Leahy has a quirky side that has softened his personal image through the years. He loves Batman comics and had a cameo role in one of the Batman movies; he is a huge fan of the Grateful Dead (I remember him returning one of my calls backstage at a Dead concert; needless to say, I could hardly hear him); and he is similarly a fan of U2. Visitors to his Washington office can't miss the photos of

Bono and Leahy. Leahy's long-time interest in and skill at photography provide a whole new dimension to his personality. Photographs he has taken during his Senate-sponsored travels reveal a man sensitive to the world's needs and universal humanity. Like Aiken, however, who spent decades in Washington but vowed he was most at home on his hill farm in Putney, Leahy seems most at home on his farm in Middlesex, despite his more than three decades in Washington.

"Take Back Vermont" signs sprang up around the state following passage of the civil unions law.

"The people of Vermont clearly don't believe what we believe."

— Ruth Dwyer,
twice Republican nominee for governor

Chapter 11

The Pulse of Politics

I n early 2001 I spoke at the Inn at Montpelier to a statewide business group about the 2000 elections. Someone in the audience asked if I saw any Republican on the horizon who could be elected governor. I thought for a minute and replied that I did not. Maybe Jim Jeffords could, I mused, but I doubted he had any interest in returning to Vermont to run for governor, the office that had eluded him almost thirty years earlier. Within minutes after I returned to my office, the phone rang. "Sooooooo, you don't think that there are any Republicans who can be elected governor," said Jim Douglas with a laugh. I was surprised that word of my comments had already made their way back to him, and embarrassed that I had not even mentioned his name.

But the truth was that the Republican Party had so marginalized itself in the elections of 1998 and 2000, and with the gubernatorial candidacies of Ruth Dwyer, that I thought years would pass before the party regained credibility with the broad middle that decides elections.

"The people of Vermont clearly don't believe what we believe," Dwyer said bitterly on election night in 2000.

As I made the comment to the business group, I was thinking about how the party had treated Dick Mallary, Marion Milne and Bob Kinsey in the 2000 election. Each of them had devoted their lives to public service through the Republican Party, and all were treated poorly. I found Mallary's decision to leave the GOP to be especially troublesome for the party's future. By turning against Mallary on the basis of his single vote for civil unions, after a lifetime of devotion to the party—fifty years in the state House and state Senate, in the administration of two governors and as a member of the U.S. House—the party had sent a message of exclusion, not inclusion.

I was thinking, as well, of the demographics of the state. According to the most recent exit polls I had seen, Vermont was the most liberal state in the nation, and election results proved that. In 2000, Gore had carried the state—as Bill Clinton had in 1992 and 1996—and Ralph Nader had garnered seven percent of the vote, one of his best showings nationally. The state's congressional delegation—U.S. Senators Pat Leahy and Jim Jeffords and U.S. Rep. Bernie Sanders—was (and still is) the most liberal delegation in the nation. Of the six state offices of governor, lieutenant governor, auditor, treasurer, attorney general and secretary of state, the Democrats held all but one: the office of state treasurer, held by Jim Douglas.

Against this backdrop, how, then, did Douglas win the office of governor in 2002? He worked the hardest, fashioned a simple and compelling message and stuck to it. From his campaign kickoff in May 2002 to Election Day in November, the Douglas message never wavered: JIM EQUALS JOBS. In politics, timing is everything, and Douglas was perfectly in sync with the events of 2002. One month after he formally launched his campaign, IBM laid off 988 workers. Layoffs occurred regularly around the state right through Election Day:

Bombardier, in Barre; Wyeth, in Georgia; EHV Weidman, in St. Johnsbury; the closing of Ames stores statewide. Every layoff reinforced the Douglas message that the state needed to do more to attract and hold industry.

Douglas also ran a perfect campaign. He threw his opponent, Democratic Lt. Gov. Douglas Racine, on the defensive from the start by running a series of ads portraying Racine as a "flip-flopper" on major issues. Douglas also painted Racine as a tax-and-spend liberal, a perception reinforced by newspaper editorial endorsements around the state.

Douglas' 2002 win was a remarkable accomplishment, but it also fit a pattern I had first noticed in 1984, and one I had written about regularly ever since then. Without fail, Vermont since 1962 has alternated Republican and Democratic governors. In doing so voters have done more than just alternate between parties: They have chosen governors so that a period of expansion follows a period of retrenchment, which, in turn, follows a period of expansion.

> From his campaign kickoff in May 2002 to Election Day in November, the Douglas message never wavered: JIM EQUALS JOBS. In politics, timing is everything, and Douglas was perfectly in sync with the events of 2002.

This unusual forty-year political pulse, an ebb and flow as voters used the ballot box to guide the direction of state government, began with the watershed 1962 election of Democrat Phil Hoff, who broke the GOP's century-long hold on the governor's office by ousting incumbent F. Ray Keyser, Jr. Hoff served six indefatigable years, transforming just about every aspect of the state's life. In 1968, however, when voters faced a choice between a Hoff protégé—his own lieutenant governor—and a conservative Republican business executive, the voters chose the GOP candidate, Deane Davis, in large part because they feared Hoff's expansions of state programs were leading to fiscal problems.

Davis cleaned up the state's fiscal affairs, primarily by instituting a state sales tax. He then began reorganizing state government and tackling concerns about overdevelopment by championing passage of the pioneering Act 250 review process. When Davis stepped down in 1972, voters again had a choice between a candidate pledging to continue the governor's policies and one promising change. This time they went with change, choosing Democrat Tom Salmon.

Salmon was followed by Republican Richard Snelling, a businessman in the Davis mold, who, in turn, was succeeded by Democrat Madeleine Kunin, who had campaigned as an activist. Snelling returned to office following Kunin's retirement, insisting that someone had to get the state's fiscal house back in order. Democrat Dean became governor upon Snelling's death, but he focused on his predecessor's fiscal concerns, so that even though he wore his party's label during the first half of his long tenure as governor, many Vermonters tended to see Dean's first two terms as an extension of Snelling's term.

> For much of the 20th century, the image of Vermont derived from the persona of Calvin Coolidge, the poems of Robert Frost, the paintings of Norman Rockwell and music like "Moonlight in Vermont."

In the second half of Dean's tenure, however, Vermont underwent monumental change more typical of Democratic expansionism, highlighted by the passage in 1997 of Act 60, a new system of financing schools, and the passage in 2000 of a system extending the benefits of marriage to gays and lesbians. By 2002 I was convinced that Vermonters were exhausted by the period of turmoil and would regard the second half of Dean's years as a time of expansion rather than retrenchment. Thus the historic pulse I had been monitoring would favor a Republican in the 2002 elections.

At the time, though, I also wondered whether the pulse was still relevant with an electorate so inclined to Democrats and so heavily concentrated in Chittenden County. Racine was from Chittenden County; Douglas was from Addison County. Every governor since 1977 had hailed from the Burlington area; four of the seven chief executives since 1961 lived in Chittenden County at the time of their election. By comparison, not a single governor from 1900 to 1960 lived in Chittenden County.

Douglas' win was a tremendous accomplishment, but it was a personal, not partisan, victory. Democratic House and Senate candidates won big in communities that went to Douglas. Incumbent Republicans lost in communities carried by Douglas. Once elected, though, Douglas moved quickly to rebuild his party and to broaden his appeal. Nothing spoke as loudly as one of his first appointments: He named Dick Mallary to be commissioner of taxes. Mallary, cast aside by the anti-civil union forces the previous year, returned to state government, more than forty years after he first won election to the Vermont House, and 36 years after he welcomed my eighth-grade class to the State House. In offering the post to the 74-year-old veteran politician, Douglas made it perfectly clear that his was again a party of inclusion.

The Vermont that Mallary served in 2003 was a different world politically than it had been when he launched his career in the 1960s. Today Douglas, too, governs a state dramatically different from the one that existed when he arrived in the state House in 1973. Those differences are most obvious in the politics, where the state's prevailing ideology has evolved from being among the most Republican in the nation to being among the most Democratic. The differences, though, are more than partisan. They represent fundamental changes in how the rest of the nation perceives Vermont.

For much of the 20th century, the image of Vermont derived from the persona of Calvin Coolidge, the poems of Robert Frost, the paintings of Norman Rockwell and music like "Moonlight in Vermont."

Coolidge, wildly popular as president, provided many Americans with their first encounter with a Vermonter. What they saw—or thought they saw—was Silent Cal, frugal, moral, steady. Rockwell's series of paintings known as "Four Freedoms" used life as portrayed in a small Vermont town to personify the freedoms that rest at the core of the country's heritage. Frost's poems conveyed the message that Vermonters were good neighbors, while the song "Moonlight in Vermont" made every listener shiver in romantic delight for a time they thought was gone.

Today people all around the country have a vivid impression of Vermont and Vermonters. But the symbols are no longer Silent Cal, Robert Frost and "Moonlight in Vermont." The new symbols are Ben & Jerry, Bernie and Jim Jeffords, the writings of Jamaica Kincaid and Galway Kinnell, and the music of Phish. They include Pat Leahy and Howard Dean, civil unions and a breathtaking landscape. Vermont is the quirky state. It's Chunky Monkey.

One thing, however, has remained constant from the day Dick Mallary stepped into the State House through to Jim Douglas' administration: Vermonters continue to believe Vermont is a special world. They still believe their leaders can accomplish things that leaders in other states cannot, and that their leaders can work across the political aisle.

That belief helped forge the compromises in 2006 between the Republican Douglas and the Democratic Legislature that led to adoption of what is considered the most comprehensive healthcare reform plan adopted by any state.

The heart of the belief in Vermont's uniqueness, though, has nothing to do with politics and everything to do with the pastoral. What joins them across farm and city, across party, across economic differences and class is a deep appreciation for all that is around them. They want to keep Vermont as it is.

Jim Douglas, in his second inaugural, captured the feeling that ties together people in every corner of this state, of every political persuasion:

> If, at the beginning, the Almighty gave to humanity a sliver of globe on which to carve a heaven on earth, it would be filled with verdant hills and sparkling lakes, open fields and forests thick with all His majesty. The joy of changing seasons would bless a people with a cycle of life and instill in them the spirit of freedom and a sense of unity.
>
> And they would call it Vermont.

Chris Graff in 2006.

Epilogue

"You're fired"

My career with The Associated Press came to an abrupt close at 9:30 a.m. on Monday, March 20, 2006. Larry Laughlin, the AP's bureau chief for Northern New England, handed me a letter that began, "This is to inform you that your employment at The Associated Press has been terminated effective immediately." In his letter, Laughlin claimed "your decision to allow an elected official's editorial comments to run unfettered on the wire March 8 compromised the integrity and impartiality of the AP's news report. That was a repeat of the failure in judgment displayed in 2003 when you were admonished for allowing a Montpelier staffer to write a chapter in a member-published book about Howard Dean, at the time a candidate for the Democratic presidential nomination."

Six months later I have trouble even typing those words. I am reminded of the lede of my first story with the AP, the one about T. Garry Buckley losing the 1978 primary for lieutenant governor, when Buckley said, "It hurts too much to laugh and I am too old to cry," except I wasn't too old to cry. My professional identity as a reporter was virtually inseparable from my personal identity. Though a husband, father and friend, I was nevertheless almost always on the job, open to anything I might pick up that needed to be disseminated. My beat wasn't just politics or crime or the environment, topics that can be controlled, to some extent; my beat was the huge, ineffable, and compelling subject of Vermont, and I had learned to be vigilant because I never knew where I might find the next story. That doesn't mean I was constantly trolling for scoops; despite what television and movies might suggest, scoops are the exception rather than the rule. Most commonly, stories are the result of keeping one's nose in the air to pick up the scent of events, happenings and developments that are or should be of interest to others. News by definition isn't neat. News cycles may be fixed, but the news itself is as unpredictable as ice-out on Joe's Pond. News happens when it does, and that meant for me during the night and on weekends, while I was sailing or skiing, while I was vacationing in Maine or burying my parents, while I was attending my children's birthday parties, science fairs and soccer games. For twenty-five years I was responsible for filing a state report every day, 365 days a year, and this responsibility, combined with my insatiable love of reporting, had made who I was and what I did almost indistinguishable.

Plus, I had worked with a passion. Hundreds of times through 27 years I spread the gospel of the AP, building and marketing a Vermont news report that I felt met the highest standards. Countless times I worked through the night, writing, reporting and editing breaking news stories. Estimating broadly, I calculate that I wrote approximately six-million words of copy about Vermont during my years with the AP, reporting on virtually every topic, interpreting, explaining, presenting and putting the news into perspective. And suddenly, on a Monday morning in March, that life ended.

My severance agreement with the AP precludes me from speculating publicly about why I was fired. Anyway, what I know is already on the public record in the termination letter, which the AP agreed to release at my request. I also know that the "elected official's editorial comments" refers to a column written by Sen. Patrick Leahy for "Sunshine Week" at the request of the American Society of Newspaper Editors. The Society organized "Sunshine Week" two years ago to combat government secrecy and bring attention to the public's right to know. The event is funded by the John S. and James L. Knight Foundation, of Miami, whose website says the week "seeks to enlighten and empower people to play an active role in their government at all levels, and to give them access to information that makes their lives better and their communities stronger." The AP is a lead partner in "Sunshine Week," and the AP national editors required the editors in each state bureau in 2005 and 2006 to develop a package of material to move on their state wires for newspapers to use during the week.

In 2005 I had a reporter put together a story on openness in Vermont government and, as part of the package, I included the column on freedom of the press that Leahy wrote that year, also at the request of the American Society of Newspaper Editors. As one of the leaders in the Senate on the Freedom of Information Act, Leahy is a natural spokesman on the topic, which is why the editors had asked him to contribute. I put Leahy's 2005 column on the AP wire with nothing but an editor's note explaining its origins. Newspapers around Vermont ran it, knowing his thoughts would interest their readers, while no one in AP management said one word about it. Last winter, as Sunshine Week 2006 approached, I again put a reporter on a story, this time on the Douglas administration's use of deliberative process to close access to documents. I included in the package of material transmitted to newspapers Leahy's 2006 column, composed once again at the request of the American Society of Newspaper Editors and accompanied by my editor's note cut and pasted from 2005. This time, after Leahy's column appeared, the AP fired me.

The book referred to in the termination letter is *Howard Dean: A Citizen's Guide to the Man Who Would Be President*, a paperback published in 2003 by the *Rutland Herald* and *Barre-Montpelier Times Argus*, two Vermont newspapers owned by John Mitchell, who sits on the AP board of directors. Those newspapers decided in the summer of 2003, when Howard Dean became the frontrunner for the Democratic presidential nomination, to quickly compile a paperback detailing Dean's years as governor. The book's editor, Dirk Van Susteren, assembled a team of reporters to write one chapter each. One of those contributors was Dave Gram, who worked for me. Others included the winner of a Pulitzer Prize, a former chief political writer for the *Chicago Tribune*, a one-time Washington bureau chief for the *Providence Journal*, and a former staff writer for the *Los Angeles Times*. The book was an even-handed look at Dean's tenure in Montpelier. David Broder, *The Washington Post* columnist known for his fairness and objectivity, wrote in 2004 about the *Rutland Herald* book: "The nine contributors have covered Dean during the span of years that he held office in Vermont—as legislator, lieutenant governor and governor. Their views are balanced—closer to the Lou Cannon model on Reagan than any of the other examples I have cited—and I could detect no personal bias in any of their individual chapters."

My firing came just after a turbulent time for us in the Montpelier bureau and me in particular, but one that did not appear to jeopardize my job. Throughout it, in fact, I felt I had the support of the AP's corporate brass in New York, even though I know they didn't welcome the attention of this particular mountebank any more than I did. People who write the news are rarely comfortable in its spotlight.

It began in January, when Judge Edward Cashman, who presides in District Court, in Burlington, imposed a sixty-day jail sentence on a man for sexual assault of a young girl over a four-year period starting when the girl was six. The judge did so because he felt it was essential that the man be enrolled quickly in the state's sexual offender program, something that was impossible under the law while he was in jail. The sentence prompted Bill O'Reilly, of Fox News, to declare war on the judge. O'Reilly devoted three weeks of his five-night-a-week television program to condemning the judge, condemning Vermont for having such a judge, and condemning the Vermont media for not joining in his attacks on the judge.

Wilson Ring covered the ongoing controversy for the AP, but I wrote a few pieces that made me a target for O'Reilly. The first was a profile of Cashman, one that detailed the judge's reputation for toughness. This is the way the profile began:

> MONTPELIER, Vt. (AP) – Edward Cashman should be the darling of conservatives: The churchgoing Vietnam vet is a former prosecutor; his two sons have served in the military. As a judge he is best known for his hard-line stands: A decade ago he jailed for 41 days the parents of a prime suspect in a rape case because they refused to cooperate with prosecutors.
>
> Conservatives, though, have turned Cashman into Public Enemy No. 1 for his sentence of a child molester, a sentence he said was designed to ensure the man got treatment but critics say is too soft.

The criticism multiplied by the thousands—whipped into a frenzy via Internet blogs—after Bill O'Reilly told a national television audience Monday night, as video of Cashman rolled: "You may be looking at the worst judge in the USA."

Cashman, 62, big, burly, balding and bearded, is the epitome of the strait-laced military man who takes especially seriously his role as a judge. Soon after he was appointed to the bench in 1982 by Republican Gov. Richard Snelling, Cashman and his wife dropped out of their square dancing group because he feared it was unjudgelike.

On January 12, after reading my profile, O'Reilly singled me out on his broadcast as he continued his attacks on Cashman and the Vermont news media:

O'REILLY: Now most Americans understand that sentence and the attitude behind it is insane, but not the print media in Vermont. Oh, no. Associated Press reporter Christopher Graff actually wrote a flattering piece this week on Cashman. The *Bennington Banner* said people like me who criticize Cashman are "opportunistic.". . . Tomorrow, Judge Cashman gets another chance to sentence Hulett to what he deserves. We will, of course, keep you posted, but I'm not very optimistic. Very few Vermont officials will now talk about Cashman. The press is hiding up there. No surprise. But even child advocates in Vermont are afraid to speak publicly. Why? I don't know. But believe me, I'm going to find out.

One of the driving forces prompting the attacks on Cashman were initial news reports that the judge, in handing out the short jail sentence, had said he did so because he did not believe in punishment. I obtained the 114-page transcript of the sentencing hearing and found that the judge had never said that. The transcript showed that Cashman had actually said, "And I keep telling prosecutors, and they won't hear me, that punishment is not enough." I wrote another story correcting the earlier, inaccurate report. Again, my story angered O'Reilly:

O'REILLY: The Vermont media also continues to prop up Cashman. Associated Press reporter Christopher Graff has written another sympathetic story on the judge.

O'Reilly continued to press his attacks, now also using his radio program to do so. One day I received a telephone call from a friend who said he had just heard that I had been pulled off the Cashman story. Was that true, he asked? I said it was not. He had heard O'Reilly smugly announce that on his radio program, as if he could claim credit for it. Apparently, one of his producers had seen Wilson Ring at one of the Burlington court hearings, and O'Reilly inferred, incorrectly, that I had been ordered off the story by AP management. The truth was that I did not cover any of the court hearings; that was Wilson's assignment. The AP's corporate communications department asked O'Reilly for a correction. I don't believe any ever aired.

News of my firing spread quickly through the state, with first word of it posted on a *Rutland Herald* blog by Darren Allen within an hour of when I learned of it myself.

> Chris Graff no longer with the AP: One of the most venerable and well-known bylines in Vermont media was silenced today, as Vermont AP Bureau Chief Chris Graff was said to no longer be with the world's largest news gathering organization.
>
> Reached at his Elm Street home in Montpelier, Chris sounded as stunned as the rest of the state's media world. "I am trying to figure it out myself," the newsman said.
>
> His boss, Concord, N.H., Bureau Chief Larry Laughlin, was in town today and all he would say was, "Chris Graff is no longer with the Associated Press."

Within the next few days my firing would be reported in *The New York Times*, *Editor & Publisher*, *The Washington Post* and in every newspaper in Vermont. At first the reaction of those in the news business was like mine, disbelief. WCAX-TV's news director, Marselis Parsons, reported the story on the air that Monday night, saying, "Politicians ranging from Jim Douglas to Pat Leahy said it is a huge loss and a complete surprise. Some AP clients were astonished by the news and intend to appeal to the wire service headquarters in New York." As the week progressed, though, the disbelief turned to anger directed at the AP, first for refusing to respond to questions about why I'd been fired, and then, as the reasons cited in my termination letter emerged, for what they perceived as the staggering irony and senselessness of the reasons behind my firing.

Newspapers rallied to my defense, with editorials praising me and condemning the decision to fire me. The *Rutland Herald* editorial carried the big bold headline: "You're fired."

> Graff and the AP's Montpelier bureau have made politicians of both parties uncomfortable from time to time, but Graff has earned the admiration of journalists, politicians and the public over the years because of something else. For one thing, he knows Vermont. Vermont is a community that takes an interest in its public affairs, and the public grew to rely on Graff's fairness, objectivity, knowledge, and dedication to community. The tone of the news coverage in a place affects the tone of public debate, shaping the political climate of a community. Graff established a tone of respect and a rare combination: seriousness and humor. Politics in Vermont remains largely respectful and focused on serious issues, in part because of the contribution he has made.

According to the *Brattleboro Reformer*'s editorial, "Graff has established himself as one of Vermont's most respected, reliable and influential journalists. That's why this newspaper and others around the state are still shocked, perplexed and angry about the AP's decision on Monday to dismiss Graff." Emerson Lynn, the publisher of the *St. Albans Messenger*, wrote to Tom Curley, president of the AP, asking how to cancel his newspaper's AP membership. Although canceling the *Messenger*'s membership would present a hardship for a paper that would now have to develop its own statewide and worldwide report, Lynn said that it "appears to be the best means by which we can register our displeasure with The Associated Press."

Newspapers and broadcast stations weren't my only source of support. Hundreds of readers, friends and people I had never met called or wrote. By mid-morning on Monday, my wife had already started to log the calls in a notebook so that I wouldn't miss any. It was especially warming to hear from dozens of former AP colleagues around the world, including some of the AP's finest reporters and writers, like Walter Mears, George Esper and Hugh Mulligan.

My daughter, Lindsay, was home from college on spring break on the day I was fired. The three of us spent the day huddled around the kitchen table, fielding phone calls, talking and comforting each other. Her eyes grew large when I took one call, and she realized that I was being asked if I had been let go for anything immoral. For a moment none of us could breathe while we contemplated the possibility that the muzzle the AP had put on me might preclude me from making the reasons of my firing clear. I had spent a lifetime separating truth from innuendo, and now I panicked that I might have lost not just my career but my reputation. It was a relief the next morning, then, when newspaper stories started appearing supporting me. I breathed much easier.

Still, by Wednesday morning I was emotionally spent. I had promised my daughter before she came home for her break that we would go skiing during the week, and finally we loaded up our equipment and headed out. Skiing together was such a refreshing diversion, that we did it again Thursday and Friday mornings. On Friday, five days after I'd been fired, Lindsay and I were just walking in the door after skiing when a friend called to ask if I had heard the news on Vermont Public Radio that the governor and the congressional delegation were calling for me to be reinstated. He said VPR had posted the letter on its website, so we went and looked. I could not believe it. The Republican governor, a Democratic U.S. senator, an independent U.S. senator and an independent U.S. representative had come together to ask Tom Curley to explain my firing and to reinstate me:

> Dear Mr. Curley:
>
> Along with our Vermont constituents, we are stunned, outraged and saddened by the summary dismissal this week of longtime head of AP's Vermont Bureau, Chris Graff.
>
> We send this letter without Mr. Graff's consent or even his knowledge, and he probably would have asked us not to send it if we had asked. But the prominence of this position, the importance of AP to our state and its communities, and the poor treatment of a prominent and

respected Vermont journalist of Chris Graff's caliber make this a matter that we cannot ignore or passively accept. We realize that The Associated Press is a private, member-owned newsgathering service, but AP's vital presence in Vermont, as across the nation, clearly propels this decision into the realm of public interest and concern. The public has placed its trust in AP and, in turn, the public expects a degree of openness from AP that has not been forthcoming. Accordingly, we expect a substantive response to our requests.

As news subjects ourselves, we have not always enjoyed or agreed with AP's coverage decisions—the same can be said by any frequent news subjects about the news organizations that regularly cover them—but we agree that, by any appropriate measure, Mr. Graff has been fair, objective, public-spirited, courageous and dedicated to the public's right to know the truth. He has been a tremendous credit to AP in Vermont and beyond. It was completely natural, for instance, when Vermont Public Television selected Mr. Graff more than a decade ago to be the permanent moderator of public television's two leading Vermont-wide public affairs programs.

There have been many reports suggesting the reasons for Mr. Graff's abrupt termination. Although we choose not to fuel speculation, we believe that if any of these reports were founded, it would represent a serious breach of trust by AP with its loyal Vermont readership. If AP wants to repair this rift, it must work to clear the air—to let the sunshine in—on this most unfortunate conclusion.

We support Chris Graff's immediate reinstatement, if that is what he would want. Beyond that, we also ask for answers to questions that continue to proliferate in the wake of this decision.

Chris Graff is the personification of the great attributes of good journalism: professionalism, courage, steadiness, and public service by honoring the public's right to know. We would like to believe that attributes like these, lived day-to-day by devoted reporters like Chris Graff, will never go out of style.

> Sincerely,
> JIM DOUGLAS, Governor
> PATRICK LEAHY, U.S. Senate
> JIM JEFFORDS, U.S. Senate
> BERNIE SANDERS, U.S. House of Representatives

Reporters called me to get a reaction to the letter, and I remarked in amazement that if my firing could bring together a socialist, a Democrat, a Republican and an independent, then perhaps it was for the good. Privately, I was overwhelmed by the letter and all it stood for. To have these four highly respected politicians of such different political backgrounds write such a thoughtful and supportive letter meant the world to me.

By then, however, I had accepted the reality that I could never go back to the AP. To work again under people who had fired me would be intolerable. They would scrutinize every verb and quotation, and it would be impossible for me not to be apprehensive. All the support I had received from newspapers, radio stations, television stations, readers, viewers and friends had taken the AP in New York by surprise; their response, if Tom Curley's reply to the Congressional letter is any indication, was barely controlled fury. If I stayed, words that had warmed me would come back to haunt me. I knew, on the one hand, that I could continue to do my job, and on the other, that it would be impossible to undo what had been done. My career as a journalist was over. In the months ahead I would grieve as if some essential part of me had been ripped away.

I mentioned earlier that Walter Mears, AP's finest political writer, had opened the Montpelier bureau in 1956. Half a century later, he still believes the best job he ever had was running the Vermont bureau. When he first told me that, I didn't believe him. I thought surely the world he had traveled in his career had given him experiences that outshone covering Vermont, but over the years I came to understand and appreciate why he felt the way he did. I could not have asked for anything better, except the ending.

20th-Century Vermont

In 1999 I decided to assemble a list of the most significant stories and influential people of the 20th century in Vermont. I worked on the list all summer, seeking suggestions from a number of Vermonters. At times I sat at my kitchen table arranging and rearranging index cards listing the possibilities. The whole process was purely subjective. There was no balloting by readers, no voting by newspaper editors; the choices were entirely personal.

People differed on what they considered the top story. Some believed the honor should go to the 1927 flood because of the scale of the disaster, as well as its impact on the state's future. Graham Newell, a former member of the state House and Senate, chose the reapportionment of 1965. The late Vermont College historian Richard Hathaway singled out the worrisome trend that appeared to be creating two Vermonts, separate and unequal, one that was prosperous and the other composed of an underclass. In making my assessment, I considered how different the Vermont of 1999 was from the Vermont of 1900, and then I tried to determine the single most important factor in causing that change. The answer to me was the interstate highway system.

In choosing the Vermonter of the century, I looked for the person who had had the greatest influence on Vermont, not the world stage. Vermonters such as Ralph Flanders or Warren Austin or Robert Frost were thus out of the running. In choosing George Aiken, I did so not because of his years as a U.S. senator, although he continued to shape Vermont from Washington, but primarily because of his years as House speaker, lieutenant governor and governor, and for his win in the hotly contested 1940 race for the U.S. Senate.

The Top 20 Stories of the 20th Century

Construction of Interstate 89 along the Bolton-Richmond line

No. 1:

New Interstates Pushed Vermont into the Modern Age

On a late November afternoon in 1960, more than 300 cars lined up in Montpelier for a drive to nowhere. The attraction was a newly opened section of Interstate 89. The drivers headed to Middlesex, exited at the end of the six miles and returned to Montpelier on the other side of the brand new, four-lane highway.

"The scenery is marvelous," raved Arnold Pellegrini, of Barre.

"It's smooth and straight," gushed Vernon Crossett, of Montpelier.

That outing may have taken the drivers nowhere, but it opened their eyes to the potential of a highway system that turned Vermont into someplace. It was a potential appreciated even at the time. U.S. Sen. George Aiken said at the 1961 dedication of a section of Interstate 91 that paved over his boyhood home, "We're on the verge of the greatest development Vermont has ever seen."

Vermont Life, the state's promotional magazine, was equally upbeat: "These highways are not only freeing motor vehicles to serve their full economic and social potential, but are also, in inevitable consequence, expected to influence the development of the state no less significantly than the coming of the railroad."

"It took us out of the sticks and put us within a day's drive of 80 million people and right in the main economic stream of the country," said Elbert Moulton, who held a variety of development posts in the state in a career that spanned several decades.

To appreciate what the interstates have done, consider this: Vermont first proposed in the 1940s that the interstate run up the western side of the state, from Bennington to Rutland, Middlebury, Burlington and St. Albans. Imagine the difference if officials had chosen that route. Instead, Massachusetts and Connecticut fought to have the Vermont route run along the eastern side of the state so the highway would serve their communities of Springfield, Massachusetts, and Hartford, Connecticut.

Construction of the 321 miles of four-lane highway was a tremendous undertaking. It began in 1957 at the Massachusetts border. The first six miles, from the border to just south of Brattleboro, opened in 1958. Twenty years would pass before Interstates 89 and 91 were completed in the state; a spur of Interstate 93 from New Hampshire to St. Johnsbury wasn't completed until 1982.

"Vermont had never seen anything like it," said Paul Guare, the executive secretary of the state Transportation Board back when the interstate was under construction. To build one 23-mile stretch of highway near St. Albans took 17,000 cubic yards of concrete, 3 million pounds of reinforced steel, 8 million pounds of structural steel, 38,000 linear feet of steel piping and 11,000 linear feet of timber piling to support bridge piers and abutments.

No. 2:

Reapportionment of the House of Representatives—1965

The longest and most emotional battle ever fought in Vermont was over apportionment of the House. The framers created a system giving each town one vote in the House. Population was irrelevant; the lone representative from the state's largest city had the same vote as the member from its smallest town. It was a system that favored small towns and rural interests, but one that seemed at odds with the principles of a representative government.

Many people made efforts to change the system. In 1849 the state Council of Censors condemned the one town-one vote method, saying it "is unequal and at war with the principles of representative governments—it is analogous to being based upon territory independent of population like that of no other state in the Union."

Nearly a century later a minority report of a commission created to amend the state Constitution also criticized the system of apportioning House members by town as unrepresentative. "By representative government is not meant the representation of rocks and scenery but the representation of people," the report said.

But it took a 1962 decision of the U.S. Supreme Court and repeated orders from a panel of federal judges to force change. In 1965 the 246 lawmakers, working in the so-called "suicide Legislature," created a new 150-member House with districts based on population.

"Vermont ceased to be Vermont," said Emory Hebard, of Glover, who chaired the special committee on reapportionment and went on to become state treasurer. "To this day," he said in 1989, "I feel it is one of the worst things we did to the state of Vermont. We really lost something."

"There was a very, very dramatic change," recalled Vic Maerki, then a State House reporter for *The Burlington Free Press*. "Following reapportionment the Legislature clearly was more activist. There was a sense when the new Legislature came in that they represented the new Vermont."

Richard Mallary, who served as speaker of the reapportioned House, said the 1966 session "was very different. The dominance of the old-timers, small-towners was gone. We had lots of people there who viewed this as being a major watershed in the state, and they were going to come there and change the world. There was a sense that anything was possible."

No. 3:

The Flood of 1927

It had been a wet fall, with October rains running 150 percent of normal. The ground was saturated. Even a storm of average intensity would have caused flooding. But this was no average storm. In the late morning and afternoon of November 3, 1927, all Vermont rainfall records were broken, with up to ten inches of rain falling in some parts of the state.

According to David Ludlum's *Vermont Weather Book*, it was as if "a cubic mile of solid water had been lifted from the surface of the Atlantic Ocean and deposited on the hills and valleys of the Green Mountain state." Eighty-four people died, including the lieutenant governor, S. Hollister Jackson. Swollen rivers and streams destroyed more than 1,000 bridges and left 10,000 homeless.

"The flood of November 3, 1927, was the greatest disaster in the history of our beautiful state," said Gov. John Weeks.

"Nothing had occurred during the history of the state which had dealt such a staggering blow to the agricultural industries of Vermont," echoed the commissioner of agriculture.

If the only effect of the 1927 flood was the devastation it caused, it would still count as one of the most significant stories of the 20th century. But the flood did more than carve a path of destruction. It altered Vermont in countless ways, including initiating a dramatic change in the relationship between towns and the state, and between the state and the federal governments.

The state took responsibility for repairs, a huge step in the expansion of state authority over local government. And although the state professed that it would rebuild without federal assistance, Vermont eventually asked for and received $2.7 million from Congress.

In addition, many washed-out railroad tracks were never replaced, changing the basis of the state's economy from railroad to highway. The flood also settled the long-simmering dispute over the paving of the state's roads, spurring on more blacktop. And it set the stage for the construction of major flood control projects in East Barre, Wrightsville (north of Montpelier) and Waterbury.

No. 4:
Election of Phil Hoff as Governor —1962

"One hundred years of bondage—broken," shouted Philip Henderson Hoff on election night 1962 as a deliriously happy crowd in Winooski lifted him on their shoulders. Hoff had broken a century of Republican rule, ousting incumbent Gov. F. Ray Keyser, Jr.

So many factors combined to make the win possible that it is impossible to find a single element to credit. Hoff was handsome, young and energetic; he was viewed in the mold of then-President John F. Kennedy, and, unlike many previous Democratic standard-bearers, he was not Catholic, long considered a handicap in such a Protestant state. But most powerful was Hoff's simple theme that a century was too long for one party to rule; it was time for a change.

The election of Stephen Royce as governor in 1854 as a Whig-Republican and his re-election in 1855 as a Republican marked the beginning of a century of unbroken rule by the GOP.

Some years in that century found Vermont nearly alone in its support of Republicans. In 1912 only Vermont and Utah supported the presidential bid of William Howard Taft; in 1936 Vermont and Maine were the only two states to vote against Franklin D. Roosevelt.

Vermont and the Republican Party bonded out of a dislike for slavery and a strong belief in the sanctity of the union of the states. Vermonters stood firmly behind the party of Abraham Lincoln, and over the years that commitment, cemented by the Civil War, was strengthened by the belief that Republican philosophy meshed well with small-town, rural life.

Beginning with the gubernatorial campaign of Robert Larrow in 1952, however, the Democrats made serious efforts to elect their own candidates. In 1958 William Meyer became the first Democratic congressman from Vermont; that year's gubernatorial contest was so close it required a recount.

Hoff served as governor for six hyperactive years. It seemed as if no aspect of Vermont life was untouched. Yet in hindsight, what stands out most is no single accomplishment, no one concrete change. What lingers longest is the spirit.

"We were proceeding on the basis that really there was nothing we couldn't do," recalled Hoff, "that we could get rid of poverty, that we could move the state along, that we could provide a prosperous and enjoyable life for every citizen. It was a very positive time."

No. 5:
Passage of Act 250 to Control Development—1970

Vermont devoted much of the century to promoting itself. The marketing campaign paid off. In 1969, though, fear rippled through the state, especially the southern half, that the marketing campaign had been too successful. Housing developments, mostly of second homes, were popping up everywhere—and, unfortunately, in places that could not handle them.

"We had sewage running right on to the highway," said Deane Davis, who took office as governor in 1969. "These developments were being built on soils that could not handle them and in numbers that could not be supported."

Davis convened a State House conference on the environment. More than 500 people attended. The governor followed up the gathering with an executive order creating a commission on environmental control, chaired by then-state Rep. Arthur Gibb, a Republican whom Davis would later describe as "a man of great personal charm [who] was well-known for his judicial and fair-minded temperament."

Out of the Gibb Commission came the framework for Act 250, passed in 1970, which established district commissions throughout the state to evaluate development projects. The law details ten criteria for reviewing such projects.

Thirty years after the commission report, Gibb said that he had no doubt that Act 250 played a crucial role in saving what makes Vermont special. "It leads to responsible development," he said. "When you think of the irresponsible development we had in 1969. . . . Thank God for Act 250."

No. 6:

Rise of the Ski Areas, Starting in 1934

Before 1934, skiers spent most of their days climbing hills. But then, on January 28, 1934, a Model T Ford truck engine was hooked to 1,800 feet of rope through a system of pulleys in Clinton Gilbert's farm north of Woodstock.

It was called the "ski way," and suddenly it was possible for a skier to spend more time going down the hill than up. The next year Wallace "Bunny" Bertram installed an electric motor that enabled the tow to carry 300 skiers an hour.

Up north at Mount Mansfield, where a librarian from Dartmouth is believed to have made the first descent on skis, in 1914, forester Perry Merrill, Charlie Lord and a crew of Depression-era Civilian Conservation Corps men were carving out the first trail cut specifically for skiing.

Skiing was becoming a big business. It owed a great deal of its growth and success to the government. The state provided much of the forestland and parkland for the ski areas and paid for many of the access roads to them.

The federal government, through the CCC, built many of the trails. Ski areas multiplied; then, faced with increasing liability insurance costs, a number closed. But those that remained grew bigger and more viable.

No. 7:
The Creation of Public Lands

Marshall Hapgood believed that mountain land "should be absolutely reserved as public property, for combined watershed, game, scenic and lumber purposes."

In 1905 he approached the federal government, offering to sell at a low price a large tract of land near Bromley Mountain. A few years later Middlebury's Joseph Battell considered donating some 30,000 acres. In both cases the federal government refused the offers because there was neither authorization nor money.

Eventually, the Hapgood and Battell parcels would become key parts of the Green Mountain National Forest, with Hapgood's parcel becoming the first to be acquired, in 1932. Hapgood and Battell were pioneers in promoting the conservation of land for the public.

At century's end more than one million acres of Vermont were protected, about sixteen percent of the state, either as state or national forest or park or because of conservation easements held by groups such as the Vermont Land Trust.

Another pioneer was James Taylor, whose frustration over the lack of hiking trails in the state led to formation in 1910 of the Green Mountain Club. The GMC created the Long Trail, a 270-mile footpath from Massachusetts to Canada that is said to be the oldest long-distance hiking trail in the United States

———————

No. 8
The Long, Slow Decline of the Family Farm

At the start of the century, Vermont was farm country. Eighty percent of the state was farmed. At century's end, only twenty percent was. The number of farms in the state fell from 32,000 in 1900 to about 6,000 at the end of the century, with fewer than 2,000 of those in dairy.

The opening of the century saw a shift in farming: The conversion from sheep, which had dominated farming in the nineteenth century, to cows was almost total, once refrigerated rail cars and later trucks could move milk far beyond the state's borders. But it was still tough for farmers to make a go of it, especially as the population grew and development pressures on their land increased.

It is difficult to generalize about agriculture in Vermont: Even though fewer cows and fewer farms exist than a century ago, milk production is up, thanks to better breeding and improved feeding.

Vermont remains first in milk production in New England, but agriculture is more diversified today. Dairy may generate 75 percent of the gross receipts, but the remaining 25 percent is widely scattered in categories as diverse as Christmas trees, cut flowers, vegetables, lamb and apples.

No. 9:

Madeleine Kunin's Election as Governor

Women from all across the country converged on the Vermont State House in 1985 to see with their own eyes the inauguration of a woman as governor of a state. Madeleine Kunin's narrow win in the 1984 gubernatorial election toppled another hurdle for women.

Edna Beard had cleared the first hurdle in 1920, when she won election to the state House, and a second one in 1922, when she moved to the state Senate.

In the 1950s, Consuelo Northrup Bailey became the first woman to be speaker of the Vermont House and the first to be elected lieutenant governor. But Bailey declined to run for governor, feeling the time was not yet right for a woman to hold the post.

Kunin, a Democrat, who served as a member of the state House and then as lieutenant governor, first ran for governor in 1982, losing to the incumbent, Richard Snelling. When Snelling stepped down in 1984, Kunin ran again and narrowly defeated then-Attorney General John Easton. She served two more terms before leaving office.

No. 10:

Chittenden County Becomes Population and Power Base

Through the 1930s, Rutland was the state's most populous county, but in 1940 Chittenden inched ahead. By the 1970s it had almost twice the population of Rutland County, giving it six seats in the thirty-member Senate.

More important than its power in the Legislature, however, was how it became home to most successful statewide candidates.

While not a single governor from 1900 to 1960 lived in Chittenden County, four of the seven chief executives who served from 1961 to 1999 lived there at the time of their election. Every governor from 1977 to 1999 hailed from the Burlington area. With one quarter of the state's voters residing in Chittenden County, candidates already known within that county started with an impressive base of support.

Chittenden County also was at the center of a dramatic change in the state economy, as the woolen mills gave way to industries like IBM, which opened a facility in Essex in the 1950s and employed 7,500 by the 1980s.

No. 11:
Women Get the Vote — 1920

It was a long time coming. As early as 1869, the Council of Censors urged that women be given the right to vote in Vermont: "After abolishing human slavery, the next great conquest of the United States over wrong and error will be to take woman from the feet of man and place her by his side."

The first bill seeking to give women the right to vote in town meeting was introduced in the Vermont House in 1884. The measure finally passed in 1917, making Vermont the first New England state to approve a municipal suffrage bill.

Then in 1919 the House and Senate passed a suffrage bill, but Gov. Percival Clement vetoed it. The following year, advocates for suffrage asked the governor to convene a special session of the Legislature so Vermont could become the 36th state to ratify the 19th amendment to the U.S. Constitution. Vermont's ratification would have provided the necessary majority to add the amendment to the Constitution. However, Clement refused. Instead, Tennessee endorsed the amendment in time for Edna Beard to win election that fall to the Vermont House.

One newspaper account said that when the 1921 House convened, Beard took House seat No. 145. "For a long time, no mere man had the courage to select seat number 146, which adjoins her. The seat stood vacant for over an hour until Horatio E. Luce of Pomfret took the dare of his fellow members and sat down beside Miss Beard amid a storm of laughter and applause."

No. 12:

The Great Depression and the CCC —1930s

The Great Depression was a blow to a state already on its knees. What few successful industries the state had—marble, granite and machine tools—began to falter.

Estimates were that about 50,000 Vermonters were unemployed in the spring of 1933 and thousands more were living in substandard conditions.

Although apprehensive of federal aid, Vermont and Vermonters embraced many of the New Deal programs. One that changed Vermont to its core was the Civilian Conservation Corps, created by President Franklin D. Roosevelt as a way to put unemployed youth to work in forests.

The original act allowed Vermont 750 openings, enough for four camps. But not many other states or municipalities had projects ready for the workers. Vermont did. State Forest Commissioner Perry Merrill was ready with a long list of projects that impressed federal officials desperate to put men to work as soon as possible.

Soon Vermont was allotted thirteen camps. By June 1934 Vermont had eighteen CCC camps and 3,600 men at work in them. Eventually, the CCC employed 11,243 Vermont men. A total of 40,868 worked in the state building state parks, highways, ski trails, and most importantly, a series of flood control dams.

No. 13:

Election of George Aiken as Governor—1936

In the fall of 1936 the nation overwhelmingly re-elected Franklin D. Roosevelt as president of the United States. Vermont was one of two states to back the Republican presidential contender. To many this was evidence that Vermont remained one of the most conservative states in the nation. But the election that year of George David Aiken, 44, as governor, spoke volumes about how Vermont was changing politically.

Aiken, a horticulturist, was a champion of the common man and an enemy of the business interests and utilities that had run Vermont for decades.

Aiken was critical of the Republican Party, even though he remained a member, complaining that it had lost touch with the "men and women who work for a living and know what a day's work and a dollar are."

In a nationally broadcast radio speech from New York City in 1938 marking Abraham Lincoln's birthday, Aiken said, "Today the Republican Party attracts neither the farmer nor the industrial worker. Why not? To represent the people one must know them. Lincoln did. The Republican Party leadership does not. The greatest praise I can give Lincoln on this, his anniversary, is to say he would be ashamed of his party's leadership today."

No. 14:

Ernest Gibson Wins GOP Gubernatorial Primary—1946

Starting in the 1870s, the Proctor family assumed a leadership role that allowed it to run the state, with few interruptions, for some eighty years. Vermonters elected Redfield Proctor, founder of the Vermont Marble Company, governor in 1878; his son Fletcher, in 1906; Redfield, Jr., in 1922; and Fletcher's son, Mortimer, in 1944. In between, most of the governors were Proctor candidates chosen from the allied worlds of industry, utilities, railroads and insurance.

In 1946, Ernest W. Gibson, a war hero with the same name as his famous father, a highly regarded U.S. senator, challenged the re-election of Mortimer Proctor. Both men were Republicans, and the fight was in the Republican primary.

Gibson ran as the radical outsider, calling Proctor's administration "a study in still life," and said it was time to end the rule of succession: "Under this rule a relatively small clique of people choose governors nearly ten years in advance, supporting them up a series of political steps to the highest office."

The irony of the challenge was that Mortimer Proctor had done a great deal to improve the state's health, welfare and education and was considered one of the state's more progressive governors.

But Gibson won the primary and the General Election in victories the *Rutland Herald* described as "a repudiation by Vermont voters of political practices and traditions that have been long established—a rebellion, not against outright mismanagement and inefficiency in the state government at Montpelier, but rather against the inertia and lack of aggressiveness of administration policies."

No. 15:

Development of the Tourism Industry

Vermont has been seeking to entice people to the state for much of its history. It was in the 20th century, though, that tourism became big business.

The official state push began in 1911 with creation of the Bureau of Publicity. Most telling was the title of its first publication, *Vermont, Designed by the Creator for the Playground of the Continent*.

In 1931 a special commission studying the state's future zeroed in on "Vermont's development as a recreational region" as offering the most promising future for the state's economy. "If industrial growth is retarded, if agricultural problems are difficult of solution, the recreational field offers a wonderful opportunity," said the report.

At the time, though, the vision focused on summer tourists. No one then could imagine that skiing would become such a major attraction and industry. Or that millions would eventually flood the state in the fall to see the trees turn color.

The state magazine, *Vermont Life*, which began publication in 1946, was just one of the many magazines, books and movies that promoted Vermont's beauty and its people, developing the image that attracted both tourists and residents, as well.

No. 16:

Effects of the World Wars on Vermont

Vermonters have always put a premium on peace, but they have been willing to pay the price to maintain it. In nearly every war in this nation's history, Vermont has paid a disproportionately high cost of the effort and sacrificed a disproportionate share of its soldiers. And so it was with the world wars.

In World War I, Vermont announced its support of the Allied cause before the nation officially joined the war. Again, in World War II, the Legislature, in effect, declared war on Germany a full three months before the country did.

More than 14,000 Vermonters enlisted in World War I; 642 died. Nearly 50,000 men fought in World War II; 1,233 died. About 1,400 Vermont women served in the Second World War.

The war was felt at home, as well. With so many men gone, women and children went to work on the farms and in industries. The Vermont machine tool industry played a huge part in supplying parts and equipment; during World War II, Springfield area machine tool companies employed more than 13,000 people.

The wars showed skeptical Vermonters that government, which began operating such things as day care, could be a positive force in their lives. But the wars also reminded Vermonters about the extent of poverty in the state. More than half of the men who tried to enlist were rejected because they flunked their physicals, many due to malnutrition.

No. 17:

Vermont Commission on Country Life—1931

For more than two years, 300 Vermonters worked to chart a better future for the state. The Vermont Commission on Country Life, chaired by former Gov. John Weeks, for the first time brought together a group of Vermonters to formally assess the state of the state and to plan for the future.

The commission reports provided comprehensive assessments of the state's people, climate, soils, agriculture, fish and game, summer residents, disabled people, educational facilities, medical facilities and much more.

Controversy tainted the work of the commission because of the involvement of University of Vermont Professor Henry Perkins, who strongly believed that Vermont would be best served through selective breeding. As the report on the committee on the human factor asked, "What of the seedlings? How can Vermont stock best be conserved and made to continue to provide its share of leaders for the nation and builders for the state?"

But to focus solely on Perkins' part in the commission does an injustice to the significance of the commission and its report. The recommendations in many areas set the agenda for the next few decades.

No. 18:

Election of Bernard Sanders as Mayor of Burlington—1981

If ever there was a harbinger of change in Vermont in the last half of the 20th century, it was the election of Bernard Sanders in 1981 as mayor of Burlington.

Sanders, running as an independent, ousted the five-term Democratic incumbent, Gordon Paquette, by ten votes. Sanders had sought office before, running for the U.S. House, U.S. Senate and governor under the banner of the leftist Liberty Union, but never came close. In those contests, he ran as the outsider, critical of the mainstream political parties, saying they cared only about the rich.

In the race for mayor, he said exactly the same things, but focused, as well, on the needs of the city, arguing that they were being ignored by a mayor who had been in power too long.

Sanders served as mayor for eight years. The office gave him an important platform, so that when he returned to statewide politics in 1986 he had credibility beyond that normally given independent candidates.

He won just fourteen percent of the vote in a 1986 gubernatorial race, finishing third, but two years later, he finished second in a race for Congress, besting the Democratic candidate. His 38 percent of the tally was just three percentage points behind the Republican candidate. Two years later, Sanders ousted the incumbent and went to Washington.

No. 19:

Rejection of the Green Mountain Parkway—1937

The idea for the Green Mountain Parkway came in 1931 from Col. William Wilgus, former chief engineer of the New York Central Railroad. He envisioned the 250-mile parkway, which would run the length of the state, as a sister to the Blue Ridge Parkway in Virginia and North Carolina. It was, in essence, a public works project that would stimulate the state economy and be a gift to future generations.

President Roosevelt, Gov. Stanley Wilson, the state chamber of commerce, author Dorothy Canfield Fisher and *The Burlington Free Press* all backed the parkway. The Green Mountain Club, the speaker of the House, and the *Rutland Herald* opposed it.

In the 1935 Legislature the parkway proposal failed in the House, 126-111, but passed in the Senate. A statewide referendum was held on Town Meeting Day 1936, and the parkway went down to defeat, 42,873 opposed and 30,895 in favor.

No. 20:

Inauguration of Calvin Coolidge as President — 1923

Hollywood couldn't have scripted a more dramatic or compelling opening to a presidency: The incumbent president, popular but facing a growing scandal, dies suddenly in California. A telegram is sent to notify the vice president, vacationing at the family home in an isolated hilltown in Vermont.

But with neither electricity nor telephone at the vice president's home, a messenger is forced to drive from a nearby town to deliver the telegram, arriving at the darkened house around midnight.

The vice president's father is awakened by the knocking; he reads the telegram and calls upstairs to his son. At 2:47 a.m., the father, a notary public, administers the oath of office to his son in a small rustic room by the light of a kerosene lamp.

This was how the presidency of Calvin Coolidge opened in 1923. It was unique: Coolidge is the only president to have taken the oath of office in his home and the only one to have received the oath from a family member. And it resonated with the voters: Coolidge's home, with no indoor plumbing or electricity, conjured up images of Abraham Lincoln's log cabin.

The inaugural ceremony seared in the minds of voters the image of a frugal New England Yankee, devoted to family and old-style values.

The 10 Most Influential Vermonters of the 20th Century

"The Governor," George Aiken

No. 1:

George Aiken (1892-1984)

When George Aiken died in 1984, people remembered him as a man of integrity and simplicity whose voice of common sense resonated throughout the world. In the U.S. Senate, where he served for 34 years, he fought countless battles for rural America. He was the prime architect of the food stamp program; he was responsible for U.S. participation in the creation of the St. Lawrence Seaway; and he could take credit for much of the farm legislation on the books today, covering such areas as rural electrification and flood control.

By the time Aiken retired from the Senate in 1975, he had acquired the status of a Vermont icon. In his final re-election bid, in 1968, the Republican reported spending $17.09, mostly for postage to thank people for circulating his nominating petitions, "which I didn't ask them to do," he said.

He had come a long way in nearly half a century of public service. In the 1930s he was the radical outsider whom the chairman of the state Republican Party criticized as "that Communist." Countless battles pitted Aiken against the Republican establishment. Every step of the way, people recognized the battles for what they were: struggles for Vermont. Aiken was the champion of the common man. The old guard knew it and feared him; Vermonters knew it and loved him.

By fighting those fights and winning, Aiken did more to shape Vermont in the 20th century than any other single person. Today's Vermont stands as a legacy to Aiken and the fights he fought.

The banks, the railroads, the marble companies and the granite companies lost their monopoly on Vermont government when Aiken became governor. The forgotten farmer, Vermont's silent and suffering majority, was dealt a new hand as Aiken gave rural residents the will and the way to survive. Farmers banded together to market their goods and formed electric and insurance cooperatives, all of which gave them new clout and new hope. "On farm after farm, whether the owner had been ready to give up, he received renewed hope, faith and income, after he obtained electricity," Aiken recalled decades after the cooperatives he helped create brought power to the rural reaches of the state.

Aiken was so unassuming and so easy-going that it was hard to imagine he accomplished all he did. His success stemmed in part from timing: Vermont's farmers were ready to rebel. However, the key to victory was Aiken: his style, his integrity, his cunning and his unwavering belief in the principle of fairness.

In those early years, between 1931 and 1940, Aiken was too often underestimated. Few of his well-financed foes realized that Aiken's folksy style masked one of the sharpest minds in the country. Even in 1940, after Aiken had served two terms as governor, *Rutland Herald* Managing Editor Jack Wettleson "regarded Aiken as a hayseed or country bumpkin who shouldn't be taken seriously," according to Robert Mitchell, then a State House reporter and later publisher of the *Herald*.

This quiet horticulturist from Putney began his political career in 1931, when he took a seat in the Vermont House. The speaker of the House, aware only that Aiken liked flowers, appointed him to the Conservation Committee. "They thought I knew all the trees and plants, but they overlooked the fact that the Conservation Committee had consideration of the streams and the waterpower of the state," remembered Aiken decades later. Aiken did love plants, but he hated the private power companies.

"The utility boys were trying to take over the state," he said. As the session opened, the speaker of the House sponsored a bill to construct eighty dams on Vermont rivers, a move designed to aid the power companies. Aiken fought the bill and won. Two years later he was the speaker of the House. Two more years and he was lieutenant governor; another two and he was governor.

Aiken had cultivated a political base even before he entered politics. He was the author of several books on fruits, berries and wildflowers, and he traveled the state on behalf of his Putney nursery. "I had been active in the Grange, active in the Farm Bureau, and I had the nursery and about 10,000 customers in Vermont, in virtually every town in the state," he once said. "Believe me, that's probably how I got elected."

The white-haired nurseryman served as governor for four years, during which he flirted with a presidential bid. As he worked to reshape Vermont, he sought to rebuild the national Republican Party, which had been devastated by the Democratic victories during the Depression. In a nationally broadcast speech at the GOP's Lincoln Day dinner in New York, Aiken set the party regulars sputtering when he said, "The greatest praise I can give Lincoln on this, his anniversary, is to say that he would be ashamed of his party's leadership today."

As enthusiasm for him grew, Aiken was described as a "5-foot-8 Lincoln." Historian Bruce Catton described the publication in 1938 of Aiken's book, *Speaking from Vermont*, as "the fuse leading to an Aiken boom in 1940." However, Aiken was cool to the prospect of a presidential bid in 1938, and two years later he ran for the U.S. Senate.

His victory in the Republican primary over the establishment's candidate, Ralph Flanders, marked the last time the old guard challenged Aiken. The next year Aiken's fight for rural America moved to Washington.

In Washington, Aiken was known as a man of modest power but immense influence, a person to whom presidents turned when they were in trouble. He was a Republican who had breakfast almost every day for twenty years with the Democratic leader of the Senate. He was a simple man who stopped daily on his way to the Capitol to feed the pigeons.

And unlike many in Washington, George Aiken held strong to his Yankee roots during his years in Congress. "I've never felt at home in Washington," he told a reporter as he prepared to leave the Senate in 1975. "No, Washington's not home. Home's up on the mountains in Vermont where I always lived."

No. 2:
Deane C. Davis (1900-1990)

Deane Davis had enough careers to fill a lifetime even before he won the office of governor. He had been a lawyer, county prosecutor, Superior Court judge and then president of the National Life Insurance Co. But in 1968, at age 67, he decided to run for governor.

Davis had never served in the Legislature nor held state political office, but he was highly respected and had considerable knowledge of state government through the chairmanship in the 1950s of a commission that had recommended a complete overhaul of state government. He entered the race as the underdog, with his age an issue, but bested then-Attorney General James Oakes in the Republican primary and consequently defeated then-Lt. Gov. John Daley in the General Election.

He faced controversy minutes after taking the oath of office in 1969 for proposing the creation of a state sales tax to help pay for the explosion in state programs enacted during the 1960s. The sales tax passed.

In 1970 Davis had one of the most successful legislative sessions enjoyed by any governor in any time. Lawmakers enacted Act 250, Vermont's pioneering law designed to control development, and Act 252, an innovative water quality law.

No. 3:
Perry Merrill (1894-1993)

Perry Merrill did more to shape the physical Vermont that exists today than any other single person. His title changed over 47 years, from state forester to commissioner of forests and parks, but the titles never meant much anyway.

As the *Rutland Herald* said in an editorial upon his retirement in 1966, "In those 47 years, Merrill literally invented a government power base that enabled him to serve through 19 governors, and allowed him a dominant voice in the state's development."

Or as former newspaper editor Steve Terry once wrote, "Merrill took over a tiny, unimportant state agency and developed it into one of the most important in the entire government complex."

Merrill has been called the "patron saint of the ski industry," and George Aiken once said, "His was one of the first cries in the wilderness for conservation—and particularly, for conservation education."

When the federal public works jobs program known as the Civilian Conservation Corps started up in the 1930s, few states were prepared with projects. Merrill, however, had a long list, and Vermont received thousands more workers and much more money than originally allocated.

No. 4:
Philip Hoff (1924-)

Sometimes someone makes history by being the right person in the right place at the right time. So it was for Philip Hoff.

The young, energetic and handsome leader was the Democratic gubernatorial nominee in 1962, and was able to capitalize on a decade of hard work by the Democratic Party in building its stature and the credibility of its candidates. Hoff also gained from the popularity of President John F. Kennedy and the unpopularity of the Republican incumbent, F. Ray Keyser, Jr.

Hoff, a lawyer, was born in Massachusetts, served in the Navy and graduated from Williams College. He received his law degree from Cornell and moved to Burlington in 1951. In 1960 he won a seat in the state House. In 1962, Vermonters elected him governor.

Hoff served as governor for six hyperactive years. He stepped down as governor in 1968, and then ran unsuccessfully for the U.S. Senate in 1970. He later became chairman of the state Democratic Party. In the 1980s he returned to politics, serving in the state Senate.

"The people of Vermont have clearly said that they don't want to continue with the old ways, and if we fail to respond to forces at work in our society, we face a bleak future," said Hoff in his first inaugural.

No. 5:

Consuelo Northrup Bailey (1889-1976)

Consuelo Northrup Bailey blazed trails for women: She was the first woman admitted to practice before the U.S. Supreme Court; one of the first women in the nation to be elected a prosecutor; the first and only woman to serve as speaker of the Vermont House; and the first woman in the nation to be elected lieutenant governor.

Outspoken and ultraconservative, Bailey never considered herself a feminist. One of her favorite sayings was, "Born a woman; died a person." But she was conscious of being first. In her acceptance speech after being elected speaker in 1953, Bailey told of when Calvin Coolidge "said he was going to appoint a woman to the United States Customs Court of New York City. He was told that no woman had ever held the post, and he replied, 'No one will ever say that again.'"

Bailey decided in 1955 that Vermont was not ready to elect a woman governor, so she decided not to seek re-election as lieutenant governor. Lola Aiken, widow of U.S. Sen. George Aiken, said she feels Bailey was right: "If she had run for governor, I think she would have been slaughtered."

No. 6:

Dorothy Canfield Fisher (1879 -1958)

From her book *Vermont Tradition* (1953):

> To those of us who live here it is as familiar and life giving as air or water, and as difficult to define in terms of human satisfaction. Can any words bring home to a reader in New Orleans or Singapore the tang of an upland October morning, the taste of a drink from a cold mountain spring? Certainly it is nothing fixed. Vermonters are fiercely unregimented....They will argue with each other and with the road commissioner hour after Town Meeting hour, about where to put a culvert. They disagree with one another more often than they seem to agree. Yet, although you can't predict exactly what they will do in any situation, you can always make a close guess as to the sort of thing they will do, and—more or less—what they will say when doing it. And what they will refrain from saying.

When Dorothy Canfield Fisher died, her associates at the Book-of-the-Month Club said in a statement, "She was more than an American of great ability. She was one of the rarest and purest character. A confirmed Vermonter, she was also a cosmopolitan in both space and time. All who knew her felt at once this combination of deep-rootedness and broad humanity; and felt themselves the larger for it."

Fisher, of Arlington, was one of the country's most popular novelists. She was founder of the first adult education program in the country and a member of the Book-of-the-Month Club selection committee from 1926 to 1951.

She also served on the Vermont Board of Education, the first woman to do so. Her novels were popular nationally: *The Brimming Cup* was the second-most popular novel in 1921 after Sinclair Lewis' *Main Street*. But in Vermont she has been known mostly for her passionate writings about the state. Fisher's *Vermont Tradition* is considered the most successful attempt to express in writing the qualities that make Vermont and Vermonters special.

No. 7:

Ernest W. Gibson (1901-1969)

Ernest W. Gibson, Jr., returned home from World War II a hero. He had been injured by shrapnel from a bomb during a Japanese air raid in the Pacific. A photograph of Gibson getting his head bandaged, blood spattered over his uniform, played prominently in national and state newspapers.

Gibson already had a strong reputation: He had served briefly in the U.S. Senate, appointed by Gov. George Aiken, following the death of Gibson's father. But a race for governor was not on young Gibson's mind. He and most others expected that even-more-famous war hero Maj. Gen. Leonard "Red" Wing would run for governor in 1946. But Wing died in 1945, and the race fell to Gibson.

Hammering away at the theme that it was time to oust from power the business interests that had run the state for so long, Gibson defeated the incumbent governor, Mortimer Proctor, in the Republican primary. The Gibson years did much to strengthen the education and welfare systems in the state. In 1950, though, Gibson resigned to become a federal judge.

No. 8:

Edna Beard (1877-1928)

When *The Burlington Free Press* ran its roster of newly elected legislators in the 1921 session, it added "(woman)" next to the name of Edna L. Beard, of Orange. She was the first woman member of the General Assembly and the only one in the 1921 session. She was an oddity among the other 245 members of the House; after she took her seat (No. 145), one newspaper reported "for a long time, no mere man had the courage to select seat number 146, which adjoins her."

But in his inaugural address, Gov. James Hartness began by noting that "It seems most fitting to begin by welcoming woman into active participation in representing our people. Woman's coming into full equality in suffrage bodes well for humanity."

Beard's first piece of legislation did seem to reflect a different perspective: The bill, which passed, provided $2 a week child support for women whose husbands were "incapacitated by an incurable disease."

Beard went on to win election to the state Senate in 1922, becoming the first woman to serve in that chamber, as well.

No. 9:

Walter Hard, Sr. (1882-1966)

Carl Sandburg said of Walter Hard's poems, "I find his Yankees more fascinating than most of the Greeks in Greek mythology. He and I are of the same school in believing that an anecdote of sufficient pith and portent is in essence a true poem. I treasure and reread his volumes."

Hard, born in Manchester, took over the family drug store upon the death of his father. Meant to be a temporary move, it lasted 31 years. He operated a bookstore, served five terms in the Legislature and wrote a weekly newspaper column for forty years.

It was in those columns that Hard told the tales that prompted *Holiday* magazine to call him "a 120-pound, leather-bound compendium of Vermontiana, a genuine, ear-to-the-ground listener who has recorded the rural wit, homespun wisdom, and often enough the stoic melancholy of his people."

Hard's poems depicted life in a small community not unlike his own Manchester. His writings detailed the stories of people who "were big enough not to amount to much" and captured the forces of change that were moving into the community where his family had lived for five generations.

No. 10:

Arthur Packard (1879-1970)

When Arthur Packard became president of the Vermont Farm Bureau in 1928, the organization had fewer than 1,000 members in just five counties. When he retired as president in 1953, the organization had more than 8,000 members in all 14 counties.

Packard was the driving force behind turning Vermont's farmers into a political force. "His belief in farm cooperatives was like a religion to him," noted an editorial in the *Rutland Herald* upon Packard's death. "And in fact he had a speech on the cooperative movement that he used as a sermon which he regularly preached in the church pulpits of the state whenever he could get a hearing."

In his autobiography, Deane Davis wrote that in the 1930s Packard "was perhaps the single most powerful political figure in the state." Davis told of one incident when he was legal counsel for the dairy cooperatives and received a phone call from Packard in the middle of the night about an attempt to derail efforts to form a super co-op.

After discussing the situation, Davis suggested a change in a law that would solve the problem, but said he doubted it could be enacted in time.

"Then I watched the smoothest job of lobbying the Legislature I have ever seen," said Davis, detailing how Packard in that single day managed to have the bill introduced, passed by the House and passed by the Senate, and then signed into law the next day by the governor.

Acknowledgments

A few days after I was fired I received a letter from Jack Crowl, of Thistle Hill Publications. He urged me to tell my story, and said he would love to publish it. "Your insight into the goings-on in this state and its relationship with the rest of the world would make a fascinating read," he wrote. Jack also appealed to my heart by noting that his firm is based in North Pomfret, the tiny town where I grew up. Jack, thanks for asking.

I have long admired the bold designs of Mason Singer of The Laughing Bear Associates, in Montpelier, and was thrilled when Jack said Mason would be designing this book. Mason, thanks for being so easy to work with.

The stories in this book have been drawn from an array of sources, primarily my memory, aided by the boxes of old newspapers, clippings, press releases, notes and tape recordings I kept through the decades. In addition I have relied on several books written by some of the main characters in Vermont's past forty years, including *All Politics Is Personal*, by Ralph Wright; *An Independent Man*, by James Jeffords; *Civil Wars: A Battle for Gay Marriage*, by David Moats; *Outsider in the House*, by Bernie Sanders; and *Living A Political Life*, by Madeleine Kunin.

239

Countless times in my career I called on two people to provide some nugget of Vermont history that I needed on deadline. Gregory Sanford, the state archivist, and Paul Gillies, the former deputy secretary of state, never failed to provide the information and the context. They are both Vermont treasures.

My thanks to my colleagues in the Montpelier bureau of the AP over the years. They shared in these stories. Special thanks to the people who brought me into the AP and smoothed off some of my very rough edges: John Reid, Jon Kellogg, Nancy Shulins and Wayne Davis. I appreciate your friendship and continuing support.

I have always made a distinction between what I do and what my wife, Nancy, does. She is a writer. I am a journalist. To me there is a world of difference, although our children and others have always considered us both writers. That difference became readily apparent as I tackled this book. Her assistance transformed my collection of random stories into a cohesive book. Nancy, thanks for your patience, and for sharing a love of Vermont and its history.

Finally, a heartfelt thanks to the people of Vermont for their generosity in allowing me to tell their stories.

Photography and illustration credits:

p. 1: Author's personal collection
p. 2: Jeb Wallace-Brodeur
p. 6: Jeb Wallace-Brodeur
p. 8: Jeff Danziger
p. 13: M.R. Iasognio
p. 14: Courtesy of Phil Hoff
p. 24: Author's personal collection
p. 42: Jeff Danziger
p. 58: Sandy Macys
p. 72: Author's personal collection
p. 96: Jeb Wallace-Brodeur
p. 114: Corbis
p. 132: Corbis
p. 152: Vyto Starinskas
p. 170: Corbis
p. 190: Jeb Wallace-Brodeur
p. 198: Craig Line Photographics
p. 211: M.R. Iasognio
p. 212: Jeff Danziger
p. 215: Vermont Agency of Transportation
p. 230: Author's personal collection